About the Author

Gundula Maria Avenali, aka Puran Sukh Kaur, has been dealing with natural sciences and spiritual teachings for 25 years. After completion of her university degree in Food Engineering and Biotechnology she was more than 10 years in business and politics.

She is the founder of the Waldzell Institute, which brought together renowned personalities from science, economics, arts and spirituality such as HH the Dalai Lama, Paulo Coelho, Isabel Allende, Frank Gehry, Christo, and various Nobel laureates engaging in a dialogue with decision makers from business and politics.

Together with her husband Sadhana Singh she founded the Waldzell Leadership Institute, which is designed to provide the wisdom of spiritual teachings into leadership and economy. With her pro-bono initiative „Architects of the Future" she supports young social entrepreneurs all over the world.

Puran Sukh is a member of the Yoga Association Switzerland (YS) and the international Yoga Alliance. She is a certified yoga teacher in Kundalini Yoga as taught by Yogi Bhajan, in Integral Yoga in the tradition of Swami Sivananda and a yogatherapist, trained in Kundalini Medicine by Guru Dharam Khalsa.

Gundula Puran Sukh Avenali

Way of the Heart

The Laws of Mind, Matter and Love

In Gratitude for the Truth
of the Timeless Teachings
SAT NAM

© 2016 Gundula Puran Sukh Avenali
Cover, Illustration: Dieter Telfser
Design: Alois Retter, Art Concepts
Photos: © iStockphoto by Getty Images
Übersetzung: Jutta Schmitt-Teiwes, JUST Übersetzung

Verlag: tredition GmbH, Hamburg

ISBN:
978-3-7345-0102-9 (Paperback)
978-3-7345-0103-6 (Hardcover)
978-3-7345-0104-3 (e-Book)

Printed in Germany

Bibliografische Information der Deutschen Nationalbibliothek:
Die Deutsche Nationalbibliothek verzeichnet diese Publikation in der Deutschen Nationalbibliografie; detaillierte bibliografische Daten sind im Internet über http://dnb.d-nb.de abrufbar.

Table of Contents

Preface...7

The Universal Laws..**11**
Introduction...11
The Kybalion..12
Hermetic Philosophy..16
The Seven Spiritual Laws of the Kybalion.............................18
    1. The Principle of Mentalism..19
    2. The Law of Correspondence.....................................32
    3. The Law of Vibration...40
    4. The Law of Polarity..48
    5. The Law of Rhythm...53
    6. The Law of Cause and Effect.....................................56
    7. The Law of Gender..63

WAY OF THE HEART..**68**
Introduction...68
The Keystone of the Pyramid...70
8. The Law of Neutralisation..71
    The Neutral Mind..78
    The Essence of True Identity...80
    The Power of NOW..81
9. The Law of Love..82
    Love – the Non-Duality...84
    The Science of Love..86
    Characteristics Of Human Love.....................................88
    Characteristics of Unconditional Love..........................89
    The Vivid Aspect of Unconditional Love......................91
    The Philosopher's Stone..95
    The Magic of the Heart..97
    The Path to Unconditional Love....................................99

A PATH OF AWAKENING 102

Mind, Matter and Love 102
The Circle of Creation 104
WAY OF THE HEART– A Path of Truth 107
A Path of Awakening 108

Practice 112

Why Spiritual Practice? 112
Important Aspects of Spiritual Practice 113
Stages of Spiritual Development 116
Place, Time and Duration 118
Meditations to the WAY OF THE HEART 120

The Law of Mentalism 121
The Law of Correspondence 125
The Law of Cause and Effect 128
The Law of Vibration 129
The Law of Polarity 131
The Law of Rhythm 134
The Law of Gender 137
The Law of Neutralisation 139
The Law of Love 141

Additional Information 144
Contact the Author 144
Bibliography 145

WAY OF THE HEART

The Laws of Mind, Matter and Love

Preface

For a long time I had been thinking whether I really wanted to publish this book. It seemed to me a bit presumptuous to add something to the heart piece of Hermetic philosophy, the Kybalion, based on the legendary emerald tablets, the Tabula Smaragdina. However, daring to release this publication it is my aim to focus public attention on this still unjustified less-known masterpiece. Also the age we have entered now, the Age of Aquarius, the time when finally the consciousness of Christ shall awake in all of us, contributed to my decision. I wish to point out that this amendment shall be a proposal of mine based on personal research and insights. I do not claim validity or general acceptance.

You may certainly want to know how I obtained insight in these two laws. To explain this, I have to reach far into the past. In 2008 I had a surgical operation after which I did not wake up and remained in coma respectively artificial deep-sleep mode. The doctors said my chances to survive were almost gone. However, there were some „coincidences"which helped me wake up again. My physical condition was extremely bad and I needed some more surgical operations in order to cope with the severe damages of the long-lasting coma. Doctors said that I would never again be able to live a normal life. Nevertheless, this did not bother me because I instinctively knew I would come back because there was another 'mission' I had to fulfil.

This mission was transmitted to me during my stay on the other levels of being. I only had to trust so that the clarity of my mind and the power of love would heal me. This was exactly what happened.

Some months after I had left the hospital and had regained some power again, I met Eveline Stalzer, from whom I could learn a lot, at a seminary where I was introduced to the Kybalion and the seven spiritual laws described therein. I knew immediately that this was my topic. Everything I got to know there was totally known to me and I experienced sublime intimacy, fascination and adoration for these laws.

This was the beginning of deep activity in this field: I read all books and literature I was able to find on this topic which, to my regret, was not much at that time. During my research I finally found out that originally there were two further laws, i.e. a total of nine, not seven. However, the two missing ones had never been written down, they had been secretly passed on in oral tradition from masters to pupils. I instantly knew that this was true and I had to find the two missing laws. During the following weeks my thoughts constantly circled around this question. I contemplated and meditated a lot about the topic. On the occasion of a walk along the Greek seaside I suddenly knew what these two missing laws must be about.

Back home, I immediately wrote them down, added the seven known laws and again contemplated intensively on them. I noticed that even the original order of the 7 known laws would not be correct. In a certain position the order had been changed; had this been done deliberately or unconsciously?

I did not know and it was not of relevance to me because I was so overwhelmed by the treasure revealing before my eyes: The new chronology and the two additional laws together formed as many as the entire circle of creation. In abundantly clear beautiful nine steps the spiritual laws showed the path how during the creative act matter is being created from the divine spirit and is then again withdrawing into the divine spirit. They also showed how duality emerges from unity, from the divine origin, and from her the variety of things as it is beautifully described in the TAO; and how it is possible to find the way back to unity from duality, i.e. polarity, by means of the two missing laws.

Frenzy of enthusiasm worshipping the beauty and perfectness of the creative act and its description in the nine spiritual laws I contacted Eveline Stalzer, who is also a well-known channelling medium, and reported on my findings. I asked her to check with her means of insight into the spiritual worlds, whether all this may be true. She followed my request and was astonished to find out that I am right regarding to both the two additional laws and to the change of the order.

During the following years I started holding seminaries on the topic. After some years I decided to publish this knowledge in a book in order to make it accessible to a larger circle of people. During these years of teaching the spiritual laws I also immersed deeply into the practice of Kundalini Yoga following Yogi Bhajan, which is a more than 7,000-year-old spiritual discipline formerly only reserved to kings in order to lift them up and to support them in their great responsibility. The incredible treasure of perfectly and highly efficient-working meditations for the transformation of consciousness offered in this spiritual tradition gave me the impulse to also present a practical path for the integration into consciousness, additionally to the theoretical knowledge of spiritual laws described in my book.

The selected meditations described in the practical part of the book were taken from Kundalini Yoga following Yogi Bhajan and will help you to obtain the described result with scientific precision if they are carried out daily during 40, 90 or 120 days.

Credits

I say thank you to all teachers who have accompanied me during my spiritual development thus preparing the path for this book. Special thanks to Eveline Stalzer, who first gave me information on the Kybalion and the spiritual laws, as well as to Guru Dharam Singh Khalsa, who was one of the first and most important teachers of Kundalini Yoga.

My very special thanks to my life companion Sadhana Singh who largely encouraged me to publish this book and gave me a lot of support during the selection of the meditations.

With appreciation

Puran Sukh Kaur, aka Gundula Maria Avenali

The Universal Laws

Introduction

One of the most crucial questions of our civilisation today is, how the modern sciences and the scientific-materialistic view of the world can be united with a spiritual worldview. This is of utmost importance not only for our personal goals and decisions in life, but also on a global level for finding a permanent solution for the variety of problems we are confronted with.

So far, there has been the opinion that there is no unity between the world view of sciences and a spiritual world view. There has not been another choice for us as to decide upon either of the paths. However, how did or how do we get along with this inner conflict? During the day in our professional surrounding we act like the rational realist, only counting on facts. In the evening, among our beloved ones, we realise that love is the greatest gift in our lives or when seeing the sky at night we have a feeling of infinite vast fascinating us leaving the problems of our daily life far behind us.

Then, at a certain point in life something really extraordinary happens: We make an experience which clearly cannot be 'of this world', an event we normally name supernatural because it is not based on our five senses. If we are really able to face this experience and not push it aside the next day because it does not fit into our well-organised life, at least then we are undeniably faced with the question of compatibility of science and spirituality, of our material and our spiritual nature.

But what are the criteria relieving us? Where can we cling to? Who can give advice? What are we searching for? What is the reason for our feeling of conflict? What deep discomfort are we going through? How many years of my life had I been searching for the goal of my life? There had been numerous teachings, wisdom and meanings I listened to, I had gathered the most spirited and knowing people around me, understanding at the same time, that all of them were finally searching for the same. Finally, I found a small inconspicuous book in my search for the 'philosopher's stone'. This is what I am going to talk about in this book...

The Kybalion

"All the fundamental and basic teachings embedded in the esoteric teachings of every race may be traced back to Hermes. Even the most ancient teachings of India undoubtedly have roots in the original Hermetic Teachings. From the land of the Ganges many advanced occultists wandered to the land of Egypt, and sat at the feet of the Master. From him they obtained the Master-Key which explained and reconciled their divergent views, and thus the Secret Doctrine was firmly established. ..... The student of Comparative Religions will be able to perceive the influence of the Hermetic Teachings in every religion worthy of the name, now known to man, whether it be a dead religion or one in full vigor in our own times. There is always a certain correspondence in spite of the contradictory features, and the Hermetic Teachings act as the Great Reconciler."

The Kybalion

They do not only reconcile religions, they also provide the lost key for the integration of a material and a spiritual standpoint, forming the connection between science and wisdom. In former times, there was no separation between sciences, religion and philosophy. Even in modern India the strict distinction of non-compatible topics is largely unknown. Back into the middle ages, a common view of these topics could be seen in Western cultures, which, however, came to an end in the Age of Enlightenment. At this point, a fragmented view of reality took place leading us to the point where we, as mankind, are now standing.

Deprived of every higher sense in our lives, we only worship the God 'money' and strive for outward and passing ideals thus exploiting our environment, our fellow mates and finally: ourselves. All this happens because we have become blind for transcendent reality and fully succumbed to the illusions of the material world. Though, life defends itself in its own manner. Like the dinosaurs were doomed to extinction when they became too powerful, subjugating all the life on earth, our systems are now collapsing. War, crisis, depression and burnout want to show us that we have to change our behaviour. Blind materialism has come to an end...

What shall we do now? Go back to the spiritualism of former times? This will certainly not be possible. Evolution never aims backward; it constantly proceeds, creating ever new options. Life always aims at further development. What we need to find is a way out of the misery, a new paradigm corresponding to the actual spiritual development as basis for new social and economical systems. Such a view of the world may root in a *spiritual materialism* or a *material spiritualism* after overcoming spiritualism as a result of the Age of Enlightenment and rejecting materialism as consequence of the actual breakdown of economic and social systems. Bruce Lipton, a well-known physician and representative of this thesis delivers a well-founded scientific and spiritual explanation in his outstanding book 'Spontaneous Evolution'.

Hermetic philosophy, thousands of years old, is able to show us the path leading to this new view of the world. The reason why it is almost unknown may be due to the fact that up to modern times it has been secretly and orally transmitted from masters to pupils. This was necessary because this knowledge clearly showed the true nature of man and that he would not be willing to become a compliant object to be degraded by clerical or any other institutions of power. Nothing could be more threatening to the iron systems of power, suppression and manipulation of the masses than this knowledge. This meant that in the past it was highly dangerous to publish it because those who dared this step were rigorously prosecuted and sanctioned by the institutions via inquisition, burning of witches and other methods, as we all know.

It is perfectly comprehensible that this knowledge was kept totally secret in initiated circles and was only given to those whom it could be entrusted to. Whom it was given had to prove himself to be worthy and had to show that he had the necessary mental maturity so that this knowledge would not be misused for personal purposes or for the disadvantage of fellow beings. Until the present day this knowledge is transmitted only in secret loges and brotherhoods like the Rosicrucians, Freemasons and other circles of adepts like the following citations from the Kybalion, the centre piece of hermetic philosophy are proving.

"But this truth is not found in books, to any great extent. It has been passed along from Master to Student; from Initiate to Hierophant; from lip to ear. When it was written down at all, its meaning was veiled in terms of alchemy and astrology, so that only those possessing the key could read it aleft. This was made necessary in order to avoid the persecutions of the theologians of the Middle Ages, who fought the Secret Doctrine with fire and sword; stake, gibbet and cross. Even to this day there will be found but few reliable books on the Hermetic Philosophy, although there are countless references to it in many books written on various phases of Occultism. And yet, the Hermetic Philosophy is the only Master Key which will open all the doors of the Occult Teachings!"

The Kybalion

"Where fall the footsteps of the Master, the ears of those ready for his Teaching open wide."

The Kybalion

"When the ears of the student are ready to hear, then cometh the lips to fill them with Wisdom."

The Kybalion

"The lips of wisdom are closed, except to the ears of Understanding."

The Kybalion

But now we are entering a new age. In this age there will be no more secret knowledge: Every human searching for it shall be able to get access to the knowledge; an age in which misuse of power and suppression would not have a chance to exist. The new age we are now entering is the Age of Aquarius. Its quality is totally different from that of the preceding Piscean Age. The Piscean Age can be characterized by secrecy, mystery, misuse of power and manipulation whereas in the now beginning Age of Aquarius traditional hierarchies are broken up and knowledge will be accessible for all, even with the help of modern technologies. As brothers and sisters we will follow our way back into unity hand in hand, in love and mutual support. This will be possible when we encounter each other benevolently as equal beings of same value on our path toward new consciousness. There will be no teachers in the common sense of the meaning as a kind of superior knowledge institutions but only companions, because now every human being has to find his own path of spiritual development. Moreover, there will be no more mediators between man and god in the new age who might serve as solely entitled messengers of divine wisdom and mercy.

There are different dates and times indicated to be the beginning of the Age of Aquarius. It is not important or relevant whether it is the year 1991, 2011 or 2012 or if we are just experiencing the transition time until the year 2020. It is a fact that the cosmic qualities corresponding to this new age are already available for us and the first signs can clearly be recognized by the collapses, breakdowns and ruptures of our old systems.

We are now learning that it is about time to reveal formerly secret knowledge and to publish the knowledge of hermetic philosophy, which has been closely guarded over the millennia. This is the aim of this book.

Hermetic Philosophy

Hermetic philosophy describes a comprehensive written composition of teachings going back to the legendary character of Hermes Trismegistus Thot. It is legendary because it cannot easily be determined by modern historical research when and how long Hermes Trismegistus had lived. Many even doubt that he really had lived once.

He is a mixture of the Greek God Hermes, the divine messenger and protective god of travellers, merchants, shepherds as well as thieves, art dealers, the art of rhetoric and magic with the Egyptian god Thot, teacher of Isis, being the inventor of scripture, specialist of hieroglyphs, the god of measurement and counting, of music, astrology, protective god of the temple libraries and author of holy writings, thus resulting in the thrice Great Hermes Trismegistus Thot. He is seen as the originator respectively the messenger of all wisdom and knowledge, especially language, philosophy, astrology and mathematics, being a teacher of all natural scientists and master of the early human race. In general, he is attributed to the period between 3,000 and 5,000 BC, however, there are different meanings regarding this.

He documented his knowledge in countless books which were enjoying special reputation so that they were kept in temples and carried along during holy processions. Even Pythagoras and Plato are said to have come across and studied hermetic writings during their journeys throughout Egypt. However, all these writings went lost or disappeared in the underground because of the above-mentioned reasons in the Dark Age of prosecution, later reappearing in secret circles here and there. This is how they were found among the Gnostics and by some busy historians who found them here and there at the beginning of the 4th century AC. These scattered writings were summed up by unknown authors into the *Corpus Hermeticum* of which the legendary *Tabula Smaragdina* is the centre piece, which also includes the *Kybalion,* summarizing the hermetic teachings in seven principles or laws.

They are known as the 'Seven Spiritual Laws' and, regarding clarity, simplicity and precision, they are an (almost) complete description of the basic principles of our Universe with its variety of appearance and form of life. A real synthesis of science, philosophy and religion can be found in Hermetics, meaning that it is a teaching or a kind of universal religion reconciling all religions and forming a concentration of the ancient wisdom of our earth.

This wisdom entered almost all spiritual traditions, from the Egyptian 22 great arcana, Kabbala, Indian Yoga to the great mysteries of the ancient world, from Eleusis to Orphics as well as to Christian gnosis and mystic. This is the reason why it is of immense value for the topic of this book. Therefore, its centre piece, the Kybalion, shall be the basis for the following description of an integrative world view, leading us into the new paradigm of the *spiritual materialism* resp. *material spiritualism.*

The Seven Spiritual Laws of the Kybalion

The seven hermetic principles on which the entire publicly accessible hermetic philosophy is based, was first published in a small and inconspicuous book by the three initiates in 1908. Even at the beginning of the last century the spirit of prosecution was so alive that the authors of this book would not show their true identity. For decades, the book had not had the recognition it deserved. It was only at the end of the last century and at the beginning of the 21st century that some few books were dealing with this topic, although they did not really offer more information than a transcript of the aforementioned book of the initiates together with some historical explanations or personal interpretations.

After a life-changing personal experience in 2008 this book has become the central issue of my research as described in the preface. During intensive meditation on the contents of the book the knowledge on two further previously unknown and unwritten laws were given to me in 2010. Along with a small change of order, these laws complete the seven spiritual principles from the Kybalion to a perfect system describing the entire cycle of creation, from pure mind to solid matter and from solid matter back to the pure mind.

Thus, this system thus also forming a path to awakening/to illumination, is named 'WAY OF THE HEART' and shall offer support for all those who want to escape from our illusionary perception of reality by finding their way back to the consciousness of unity with all beings and realisation of our highest human potential.

The seven hermetic principles described in this chapter are the following:

1. The law of mentalism

2. The law of correspondence

3. The law of vibration

4. The law of polarity

5. The law of rhythm

6. The law of cause and effect

7. The law of gender

"The Principles of Truth are Seven; he who knows these, understandingly, possesses the Magic Key before whose touch all the Doors of the Temple fly open."

The Kybalion

1. The Principle of Mentalism

"THE ALL is MIND; The Universe is Mental."

The Kybalion

This principle embodies the truth that "All is Mind." It explains that THE ALL (which is the Substantial Reality underlying all the outward manifestations and appearances which we know under the terms of "The Material Universe"; the ''Phenomena of Life"; "Matter''; ''Energy''; and, in short, all that is apparent to our material senses) is SPIRIT, which in itself is UNKNOWABLE and UNDEFINABLE, but which may be considered and thought of as AN UNIVERSAL, INFINITE, LIVING MIND. It also explains that all the phenomenal world or universe is simply a Mental Creation of THE ALL, subject to the Laws of Created Things, and that the universe, as a whole, and in its parts or units, has its existence in the Mind of THE ALL, in which Mind we "live and move and have our being." This Principle, by establishing the Mental Nature of the Universe, easily explains all of the varied mental

and psychic phenomena that occupy such a large portion of the public at-
tention, and which, without such explanation, are non-understandable
and defy scientific treatment.

The Kybalion

The first law is the primary and basic principle because it is the fundament all major religions and wisdom teachings and the other six laws of the Kybalion are based upon. The principle of mentalism, deriving from 'mens' ('mind') is described as follows in the Kybalion:

The All is mind in the sense of 'spirit' and the universe is mental in the sense of 'spiritual' which means that everything that is, is spirit/mind because in the Kybalion the All is defined as 'Everything that is', the primary source of all being, in the religions called 'God'. The denomination 'God' is not used in the Kybalion because it is explicitly not defined as religion. One standpoint in the Kybalion is that this knowledge, as soon as it is pressed into certain forms and rites and is institutionalised, it starts freezing which we can see in all great religions today. They are petrified and lost in their rites, while living knowledge is no longer inherent, except for the mystic traditions which, however, are not being passed on to the public.

If the All is everything that is, and if the All is of mental/spiritual nature, this means that everything that is, ever was and ever will be is of mental/spiritual nature: all kind of matter, every thought, every feeling. We all are made of pure spirit. We already are a creation which means that we are no longer pure mind but of mental nature. The above-cited aphorism from the Kybalion says that we are the universe which is a creation of the All. It says, the universe which was created by the All is mental. This means that the universe is no longer the encompassing, pure mind bearing the potential for everything in it; it is even more as it is already part of the universe created from the omnipotent all. We can compare this with a human stem cell having the potential to become any part of the body while a differentiated body cell can only become skin, hair, heart or kidney. We are thus part of the universe living in the universe created together with it through the mind of the All.

The first principle helps us to recognize what it means that everything is mental and how matter can be created from this by way of mental creation of the pure mind. We may even check this referring to our own daily life. Everything we are transforming into matter is following a mental plan. If we want to build a house there must be an architect who virtually already sees this house, i.e. somebody who already has a mental plan of it. The same applies to all other areas: Before anything is created physically, there is a mental plan of it. There is nothing on the level of matter that can be created unless it has not already been created mentally.

By implication, this is also the first key to the creation of the desired reality. If I am aiming at something on the material level I must create a mental plan, a mental picture, and an imagination beforehand. If I do not know what I want, I will not be able to create such a picture. The more concrete and vivid I can imagine the object I am aiming at, the easier, faster and more exact will I be able to create it. This also throws a completely different picture on the scorned daydreaming or fantasising of children which is of course a highly useful, even necessary prerequisite for the realisation of the relevant desire.

The precise starting point described in this first law is the fundament of the entire hermetic philosophy and all religions and spiritual teachings in the world, stating that the source/God from which every matter came from is pure mind. This mind creates all universes and every life that comes into existence. Everything created by the All thus is no longer reality itself but a creation of the last reality lying behind all this. It is thus transient, contrary to the pure mind, the source of all creation which is everlasting because it is everything meaning that there is nothing it might have come from.

God and the All

As this first law is the basis on which all other laws are based on and it finally is the only principle that has not been recognised by modern sciences I wish to cite some original quotations from the book of the three initiates, explaining which intellectual concepts and rational conclusions of our forefathers have lead to the recognition of this law within the hermetic teachings.

"Under, and back of, the Universe of Time, Space and Change, is ever to be found The Substantial Reality -the Fundamental Truth."

Man considering the Universe, of which he is a unit, sees nothing but change in matter, forces, and mental states. He sees that nothing really IS, but that everything is BECOMING and CHANGING. Nothing stands still-everything is being born, growing, dying-the very instant a thing reaches its height, it begins to decline-the law of rhythm is in constant operation-there is no reality, enduring quality, fixity, or substantiality in anything - nothing is permanent but Change. He sees all things evolving from other things, and resolving into other things-a constant action and reaction; inflow and outflow; building up and tearing down; creation and destruction; birth, growth and death. Nothing endures but Change. And if he be a thinking man, he realizes that all of these changing things must be but outward appearances or manifestations of some Underlying Power-some Substantial Reality. All thinkers, in all lands and in all times, have assumed the necessity for postulating the existence of this Substantial Reality. All philosophies worthy of the name have been based upon this thought. Men have given to this Substantial Reality many names-some have called it by the term of Deity (under many titles); others have called it "The Infinite and Eternal Energy''; others have tried to call it "Matter"-but all have acknowledged its existence.

We accept and teach the view of the great Hermetic thinkers of all times, who assert that the inner nature of THE ALL is UNKNOWABLE. This must be so, for naught by THE ALL itself can comprehend its own nature and being. The Hermetists believe and teach that THE ALL, "in itself," is and must ever be UNKNOWABLE. They regard all the theories, guesses and speculations of the theologians and metaphysicians regarding the inner nature of THE ALL, as but the childish efforts of mortal minds to grasp the secret of the Infinite. Such efforts have always failed and will always fail, from the very nature of the task.

"In its Essence, THE ALL is UNKNOWABLE."

"But, the report of Reason must be hospitably received, and treated with respect."

The human reason, whose reports we must accept so long as we think at all, informs us as follows regarding THE ALL, and that without attempting to remove the veil of the Unknowable:

(1) THE ALL must be ALL that REALLY IS. There can be nothing existing outside of THE ALL, else THE ALL would not be THE ALL.

(2) THE ALL must be INFINITE, for there is nothing else to define, confine, bound, limit or restrict THE ALL. It must be Infinite in Time, or ETERNAL, it must have always continuously existed, for there is nothing else to have ever created it, and something can never evolve from nothing, and if it had ever "not been," even for a moment, it would not "be" now, it must continuously exist forever, for there is nothing to destroy it, and it can never "not be," even for a moment, because something can never become nothing. It must be Infinite in Space-it must be Everywhere, for there is no place outside of THE ALL, it cannot be otherwise than continuous in Space, without break, cessation, separation, or interruption, for there is nothing to break, separate, or interrupt its continuity, and nothing with which to "fill in the gaps." It must be Infinite in Power, or Absolute, for there is nothing to limit, restrict, restrain, confine, disturb or condition it-it is subject to no other Power, for there is no other Power.

(3) THE ALL must be IMMUTABLE, or not subject to change in its real nature, for there is nothing to work changes upon it; nothing into which it could change, nor from which it could have changed. It cannot be added to nor subtracted from; increased nor diminished; nor become greater or lesser in any respect whatsoever. It must have always been, and must always remain, just what it is now - THE ALL - there has never been, is not now, and never will be, anything else into which it can change.

THE ALL being Infinite, Absolute, Eternal and Unchangeable it must follow that anything finite, changeable, fleeting, and conditioned cannot be THE ALL. And as there is Nothing outside of THE ALL, in Reality, then any and all such finite things must be as Nothing in Reality.

(4) Matter cannot manifest Life or Mind, and as Life and Mind are manifested in the Universe, THE ALL cannot be Matter, for nothing rises higher than its own source-nothing is ever manifested in an effect that is not in the cause-nothing is evolved as a consequent that is not involved as an antecedent.

And then Modern Science informs us that there is really no such thing as Matter-that what we call Matter is merely "interrupted energy or force," that is, energy or force at a low rate of vibration.

"Then," you ask, "do you mean to tell us that THE ALL is LIFE and MIND?" Yes! and No! is our answer. If you mean Life and Mind as we poor petty mortals know them, we say No! THE ALL is not that! "But what kind of Life and Mind do you mean?" you ask. The answer is "LIVING MIND, as far above that which mortals know by those words, as Life and Mind are higher than mechanical forces, or matter-INFI-NITE LIVING MIND as compared to finite Life and Mind." We mean that which the illumined souls mean when they reverently pronounce the word: "SPIRIT!"

"THE ALL creates in its Infinite Mind countless Universes, which exist for aeons of Time — and yet, to THE ALL, the creation, development, decline and death of a million universes is as the time of the twinkling of an eye."

The Kybalion

"The Infinite Mind of THE ALL is the womb of Universes."

The Kybalion

*Following the Principle of Correspondence, we are justified in consid-
ering that THE ALL creates the Universe MENTALLY, in a manner akin
to the process whereby Man creates Mental Images. And, here is where
the report of Reason tallies precisely with the report of the Illumined, as
shown by their teachings and writings.*

*The true teaching is that THE ALL, in itself, is above Gender, as it is
above every other Law, including those of Time and Space. It is the Law,
from which the Laws proceed, and it is not subject to them. But when
THE ALL manifests on the plane of generation or Creation, then it acts
according to Law and Principle, for it is moving on a lower plane of Being. And consequently it manifests the Principle of Gender, in its Masculine and Feminine aspects, on the Mental Plane, of course. .... You speak
of the Fatherhood of God, and the Motherhood of Nature – of God, the
Divine Father, and Nature the Universal Mother – and have thus instinctively acknowledged the Principle of Gender in the Universe.*

*But, the Hermetic teaching does not imply a real duality – THE
ALL is ONE – the Two Aspects are merely aspects of manifestation.
The teaching is that The Masculine Principle manifested by THE ALL
stands, in a way, apart from the actual mental creation of the Universe.
It projects its Will toward the Feminine Principle (which may be called
"Nature") whereupon the latter begins the actual work of the evolution
of the Universe, from simple "centres of activity" on to man, and then on
and on still higher, all according to well-established and firmly enforced
Laws of Nature. If you prefer the old figures of thought, you may think of
the Masculine Principle as GOD, the Father, and of the Feminine Principle as NATURE, the Universal Mother, from whose womb all things
have been born.*

In Yoga, the two most important philosophy systems derived
from this first law, although, from a superficial view, they seem to
conflict each other: The *Advaita Vedanta*, dealing with the distinction

of what is real and what is unreal, what is the All and what is part of the universe. Advaita Vedanta therefore is called knowledge about the non-duality. 'Dvaita' means duality, the dual principle while 'Advaita' means 'non-duality', characterizing a non-dualistic path, a path claiming one single arch-principle being the basis of all being. 'Vedanta' means 'end of knowledge' or even 'highest knowledge'.

As this material is not easily comprehensible for the human brain, Advaita Vedanta is working with metaphors which also pave the way for a better understanding. Famous examples for this are clay and clay pot. What is real? Clay or clay pot? The clay pot is unreal because his breaking means that it does no longer exist while in the case of clay, i.e. the substance, we can say that it still exists even after breakage of the form. The pot would not exist without the clay; however, the existence of the clay is not interfered by the absence of the pot. In the sense of Advaita Vedanta everything that is transient is described as unreal and everything that is intransient is described as being real. This is the way it is described in the great yoga philosophy of Advaita Vedanta, this is the way it is described in hermetic philosophy and this is the way it can finally help us to discover a new perspective on all of our material belongings including our own material bodies.

In contrast to Advaita Vedanta, the second great philosophical system of India, the Samkhya is described as a dualistic system because it postulates two basic items from which all being have come from: Purusha and Prakriti. Purusha is the aspect of consciousness inspiring - matter and being expressed only by matter. Purusha is static, immovable, resting in itself; giving sentience and consciousness to all beings. There are countless Purushas; in every being there is a Purusha as core of the being. Prakriti is the principle of nature which, however, is unconscious, unanimated. Prakriti is the creative power behind all psychophysical and material circumstances of the being including physical appearance, processes of thinking and perception. It is of divine nature, being the basis of all creation and the results of the creation process. While there are many Purushas there is only one Prakriti.

By means of the above-mentioned explanation of the principle of mentalism these two incompatible philosophical Indian systems can be united. The linking aspect is the moment where the All is revealed in the plan of creation thus manifesting the principle of gender in its male and female aspect, of course on the mental basis. However, the male principle manifested by the All is standing aside from the real mental creation of the universe itself. It only projects its will on the female principle, on nature, upon which it starts the proper evolution of the universe. This way, Advaita Vedanta and Samkhya can be reconciled by the principle of gender on the basis of the All if it is revealed on the basis of creation.

We learn that the All is reality, the all-comprising, the superior instance; there is nothing outside it, and the All/the mind is existing in everything. There is nothing where there is no mind, no being, no cell and no single grain. All and everything is permeated by the mind and mind is present everywhere. In our everyday-life this knowledge helps us to distinguish as to what is real and thus perishable, i.e. only phenomena. This especially applies to decisions which are difficult to make or (painful) experiences which we do not understand because we do not see a sense behind them. According to the above principle there is always a truth behind all these outside appearances.

When we start to ask for the truth lying behind the (uncomfortable) situation we are currently experiencing we are easily able to learn from it. Then we begin to comprehend the sense behind it and start seeing the truth as it is and not how we perceive it on the basis of the traumatic events experienced back in our past like they are stored in our sub-consciousness. So we are able to see a sense in everything, be it even uncomfortable and painful, and we are able to approach the decisive information in our lives and for our spiritual development. Easiness never before imagined finds its way into our life because we are now able to much better cope with the daily circumstances of our lives because we are now able to see the (higher) sense in them and our lesson to learn.

The outward appearance, the visible and perceptible things we are also calling matter and (only) reality, can, on one hand, be described as unreal because they are perishable as we could learn from the example of the clay pot. On the other hand, it is exactly this material reality that is considerably defining your human sphere of experience. It is of utmost importance that we do accept this reality how it is and do not deny it because we know that it is definitely not the final reality. For us, fleshly/material humans who are part of the illusion ourselves, it is forming our reality and should not be underestimated. It would only lead to a passive and fatal attitude towards our life where we would no longer be playing an active part and thus inevitably lead to failure.

This is the reason why it is important to gain consciousness about the fact that every matter in the sense of transience is unreal and illusionary because all these forms of life are exposed to vanishing and destruction. If our entire human happiness and striving depends on these illusions, we identify too much with our belongings, our body and soul, our friends and companions and we will inevitably experience sorrow and pain. Our attention should always be aiming at the everlasting reality which cannot be destructed or be part of the circle of life and death. Aiming on what will be everlasting, through all the times and in eternity. By means of the soul aspect we have access to this fine vibration penetrating everything which we call -'god'. We should always be aware of the well-being of our soul as it is our steady companion; independent from what is happening outside or which external shape we will take.

We learn that it is important for us that we finally recognise the unreal as being the relevant reality where we are allowed to make experiences as human beings because unless we accept and understand them we are able to match the challenges and move on to superior tasks. Furthermore, we must always keep in mind that this form of reality is mortal and we should not get stuck on it but set our eyes firmly on 'God' on the eternal, the imperishable. We should be aimed at the impressions of our soul which is the only one who is able to guide us to eternal happiness, everlasting joy and deep liveliness. We are thus experiencing an inner radiation power praising every situation of life, lifting it up, not knowing any limitation, recognising the divine activity, lifting up everything that may even seem profane to an act of holiness.

This leads us to alchemy which is explicitly mentioned in the Kybalion. Alchemy is defined as the possibility to transform or to refine something from one condition into another. In the sense of Hermetics the meaning of alchemy is based in the mastering of the spiritual forces; it was not about the control of the material elements. Hermetic Alchemy meant transmutation of mental vibrations and not transformation of one metal into another. The legend of the 'philosopher's stone' transforming dirty metal into gold was an allegory of hermetic philosophy what the initiates had always understood. However, it was taken literally by the common people.

Hermetic Alchemy teaches us how to transform our normal ego-consciousness, which is bound to the identification with all matter and thus bound to suffering, into a higher consciousness which means a superior vibration where we do not suffer anymore. This superior vibration more and more becomes a vibration of love, approaching more and more our true immortal core, our divine nature which is our origin. When we finally have become godlike beings we are really in a position to talk about refinement of our lower nature. Practically, this means we enter a higher vibration frequency thus transforming our life by a radical change.

'Within us is the soul of the whole, the wise silence,

The universal beauty, the eternal One.'

Ralph Waldo Emerson

It must be mentioned that 'matter' in the hermetic sense means energy, power, electricity, light, i.e. all physical quantities, as all forms of being are manifestations of creation. This also applies to thoughts and emotions, they belong to the sphere of creation and thus to changeability although they have higher frequencies than solid matter. The further and more refined the vibration of matter is, the easier it is to change it mentally because it is closer to the all-comprising mind.

From solid matter to fine matter, everything has its part of matter. Everything that has manifested like doctrines, patterns of behaviour and especially dual points of view is part of matter. Mental alchemy deals exactly for the purpose of changing unusable doctrines into usable ones.

As already mentioned above, dealing with spiritual topics may imply that we might become arrogant because we think that everything is illusion and therefore we do not take things too seriously. This seems to be in contradiction to the relative unreality and the Kybalion calls it 'divine paradox', explicitly warning of approaching this topic too superficially. In the following you may read a picturesque text taken from the book of the three initiates:

"The half-wise, recognizing the comparative unreality of the Universe, imagine that they may defy its Laws — such are vain and presumptuous fools, and they are broken against the rocks and torn asunder by the elements by reason of their folly. The truly wise, knowing the nature of the Universe, use Law against laws; the higher against the lower; and by the Art of Alchemy transmute that which is undesirable into that which is worthy, and thus triumph.

Mastery consists not in abnormal dreams, visions and fantastic imaginings or living, but in using the higher forces against the lower — escaping the pains of the lower planes by vibrating on the higher. Transmutation, not presumptuous denial, is the weapon of the Master."

We must understand that we are in a position to change all our spiritual, psychical and physical circumstances by changing our basic spiritual doctrines. We will recognize that everybody, every one of us is a deliberate part of the universe, a deliberate creation of the All although we may feel small, unimportant and helpless. Every soul has its personal, individual task in this life and plays an important roll on the big stage of life, the universe. Every soul incarnating as a human being, i.e. becomes flesh (lat. incarnatio = 'becoming flesh') has the potential to manage the challenges she is faced with and for further development, to pass the steps of life fulfilling higher and higher tasks. In reality, we are never overstretched even though it looks as if it were the case. The things we encounter are in a precise relation to our inner potential.

Moreover, there is something particularly comforting in this wisdom as the three initiates are talking about:

"So, do not feel insecure or afraid — we are all HELD FIRMLY IN THE INFINITE MIND OF THE ALL, and there is naught to hurt us or for us to fear. There is no Power outside of THE ALL to affect us. So we may rest calm and secure. There is a world of comfort and security in

this realization when once attained. Then "calm and peaceful do we sleep, rocked in the Cradle of the Deep" – resting safely on the bosom of the Ocean of Infinite Mind, which is THE ALL. In THE ALL, indeed, do "we live and move and have our being."

This is why it is of utmost importance to see the deep sense of all our experiences, although they may be very painful and in total contradiction to everything we see in ourselves. To accept them as part of our lives and to understand that we were the ones who created them in order to learn from them (despite and even because of the pain they are causing) and in order to help us to further develop. Unless this process of awareness starts we have the possibility of significant progress in our work. As long as there are experiences and areas in our lives in which we see ourselves as victims and 'innocent' (we will talk about this term later) there will not be any further spiritual development in our lives and we thus will not be able to discover the true meaning of our lives.

Everything is energy and energy is ever changeable and can be refined in the sense of spiritual development! Like it is said in the slogan of the freemasons: 'Know thyselves - improve yourself - refine yourself.' This way we are able to gain higher consciousness, a new quality of human being not only serving ourselves but helpful for our entire environment, to all of us. To the extent man recognizes the existence of the immanent spiritual being; he ascends the spiritual ladder of life. This is the true meaning of spiritual development: the insight and imagination of the vivid mind in us. This definition of spiritual development reveals the truth of every true religion.

2. The Law of Correspondence

"As above, so below; as below, so above."

The Kybalion

About the Law of Correspondence the three initiates tell us:

"The great Second Hermetic Principle embodies the truth that there is a harmony agreement, and correspondence between the several planes of Manifestation, Life and Being. This truth is a truth because all that is included in the Universe emanates from the same source, and the same laws, principles, and characteristics apply to each unit, or combination of units of activity, as each manifests its own phenomena upon its own plane."

The law of correspondence says that there is an analogy between the different levels of being. Here, the rough material sphere is the most well-known to us on the level of physical material aspects. The following higher-vibrating mental level is the level comprising our feelings, thoughts and other fine physical energies, all those of which we are unable to grasp directly. The next level, the soul level has a very high and fast vibrational frequency. The difference between these three large levels, which can also be subdivided into several further levels, is only their vibrational frequency.

These precisely separated divisions only serve for a better understanding; however, they are arbitrarily because in reality they are a continuum. The truth is, there is no clear separation between them as to where one level ends and the other begins. This, to a certain extent, is arbitrary.

On closer inspection more and more subdivisions can be found. For example the material, physical level is further subdivided in the area of human world, animal world and plant world the levels of which are further subdivided in the Kybalion for a closer recognition of the different forms of being. This is done in a scientific way just like atoms are subdivided in ever smaller sub-levels and sub-atom particles while, however, in this case the scientists hope to find the smallest of elementary parts which builds up matter.

For us, the law of correspondance has a very high practical value because observing and understanding laws on one level (especially with our physical senses or measuring devices) means understanding the principle on other levels which we are unable to directly grasp or measure with our senses or appliances. This applies for example to the vast spiritual level of the cosmos and all that is happening in the macrocosmic area and the various small levels of the microcosm which are not accessible directly, but we are able to gain insight by means of the principle 'as above so below'. Accepting these analogue laws and principles we find out about hidden secrets.

Even in our personal everyday life the law of correspondance helps us to understand all outside appearance, everything in our lives which happens to us, every stroke of fate shows us direct resonance to our innermost, our spiritual attitudes, whether they can consciously be referred to or not. By means of the outside world, we are now able to get insight in our inner world. Like all spiritual laws presented here, this law is a limitless working universal law, applicable everywhere and valid without exception on all levels and all areas at any time. There is no exception from the rule here because this would end in terrible chaos in the universe. Although it is often inconvenient to us it says undoubtedly that every event happening to me on the outside is a mirror of my innermost and shows me what I am (still) not able to learn or what I do not want to learn.

Once I have fully internalised this principle in its universal value it may become the greatest and most important teacher of my life; a guide standing at my side presenting the key for a solution, for insight at any time. As a universally valid law it comprises the huge area of human (sub-) consciousness, an area which even with scientific medical and psychotherapeutic methods can hardly be entered. This easy principle helps us getting along with things, otherwise almost impossible to achieve. The only thing necessary here is a clear mind and the courage to even face the darkest corners of our sub-consciousness.

What do, for example, my outer circumstances tell me about my-self? What are the lessons we have to learn when we get annoyed about everyday stuff and literally get worried about it; if we get annoyed about a colleague, our partner, our children or any other person, if we are impatient, stubborn, annoyed and dogmatic or bossy? Why do we always blame external circumstances? Why do we not accept the opinions of others or smile about them? Why don't we esteem each other? Why should our opinion always be the one which is correct? If we took time to think about it we would find out that the secret wish of gaining power over our counterpart is behind all that. My ego, my persona is always more important than that of the fellow human being. In reality, our environment is only a 'mirror' of our self while we are gaining awareness and visibility of our attitude only via our fellow human beings. This principle can of course be found in all spiritual teachings as for example in Yoga as the biggest of the four Maha Vakyas, the four great wisdom teachings, saying that: *'Tat Tvam Asi'* – *'This is you.'*

We can safely assume that if something on the outside is disturbing us, there is confusion inwardly. Be it because of unsolved or repressed emotions, experiences of the past, fear, jealousy or unlived need, unsatisfied wishes and desires, low self-confidence, some lack within us which we seem to recognize on the outside.

Whatever it may be, the answer can always and only be found within us. The feeling of deficiency and of making sacrifices is only an artificially created consciousness. It does not serve us and it is about time to change it into a consciousness of plenitude, recognizing that everything we need is there. The key to a life in harmony, happiness and vividness lies within ourselves. We do not need anything from the outside; we only need to change our inner attitudes, doctrines and unconscious energies in order to get all the things we deeply wish to have. The necessary insight can only be obtained by the law of correspondance; we must learn to read the book of life and to have the courage to face things, not to shift the blame onto each other, when things turn out to be unpleasant.

When we consciously apply the principle 'as above, so below - as inside, so outside', get insight in it and accept it we get access to ourselves without the mirror of our environment (our fellow beings) which would not be obvious in this form. We mostly see the faults coming from the outside because we are unable (or unwilling) to recognize the patterns of pain and suffering in ourselves.

If I really get upset of something another person is presenting to me and I am annoyed I can be sure that this has to do with a still powerful and unsolved shadow in ME! This means that it is my topic, my problem and my counterpart is only the tool reflecting it to me. In this respect this is why I should be deeply grateful for that person acknowledging him as a great teacher for me. Even if this is very difficult for us at the beginning, it will become easier the more we practise and it also changes the topic 'guilt' in our lives, giving it a completely new meaning. However, we will deepen these aspects when discussing the next law.

Of course, this principle also applies for the reverse situation if we are the tool for our counterpart and he is extremely embarrassed about our behaviour. Then it is his problem and we do not have to feel guilty for that. It is of utmost importance to clearly distinguish here: Is there something I have to change and to learn from or am I only a reflection space for my counterpart from which he has to learn something. It is not about changing ourselves to please others or to meet their expectations. It is more important that we are in harmony with ourselves and content with us. I cannot be disappointed anymore, if I do no more expect anything from others.

Practical application of this law has many aspects, even sciences often apply this principle as for example alternative medicine, homeopathy, astrology, all of them are based on this principle. One example regarding astrology: By the observation of the stars how and in which angle the planets are arranged to each other in the moment of our birth determines the birth chart which allows conclusions on our personality. The human being is the exact picture of the macrocosmic universe. We cannot find anything on the outside which would not also be present as an analogy in our innermost and vice versa. This is the reason why the temple of Delphi said: '*Know thyself so that you may know God.*'

There is great potential behind this wisdom. There is so much to discover within ourselves, we are as endless as the All itself. The second law gives us a position to find out about ourselves by means of the outside facts. This is of utmost invaluable importance. We are thus able to immediately obtain insight in ourselves, without meditation or any other special spiritual practices, directly standing in our everyday life; each and every day. It means so much easiness when we are ready to approach our true self bit by bit. Only if we are one with ourselves we can pave our way for a stepwise refinement of the world. This is the real school of life.

From the fractal structures in nature we can perfectly learn a lot about the principle of correspondence. On a tree, we see for example that every single leaf has the same structure as the tree itself. The entire information on a human being is included in every single cell.

There are even more examples in nature showing the universal law 'as above, so below' or 'as in the big world, so in the small world.' to understand it.

Our well-being also reveals the material-spiritual correspondences: If there is physical disorder, when we are ill or feel uncomfortable we can be sure that there is also disorder on the mental level. Disharmony on the physical level means that we have to search the reason for it on the mental level, thus eagerly checking all levels. As soon as we go in-depth and find out about the hidden sickening mental causes we experience holistic harmony and can return to our former salvation.

We want to be loved. We want attention and recognition. We claim to be lovable because of outside achievements. This pattern already gets started at young age: If I am obedient, neat, not giving reason for negative attention at school, getting good grades, parents and teachers are satisfied with me. They praise and love me. Thus, often well-rehearsed patterns are established, fixed dogmas which are often reflected as uncomfortable experiences on the outside.

These doctrines also arise if children ever again are confronted with the same accusations, statements and criticisms like 'You are not talented, you are not gifted, it is hopeless.' or even 'Your are always ill, your immune system is too weak, you will never ever be a sportsperson.' You will be clearly aware of the reaction these words will provoke in you. Imagine a trustful, naive child without prejudice and how deep these false doctrines become rigid patterns leading to lifelong emotional lacks and deficiencies.

In order to be accepted and loved by the outside world we are always ready to obey a lot of things. In the worst case scenario we loose ourselves, our true self, becoming adapted individuals, who align their expectations to those of the others. We are no more authentic and spend the rest of our lives searching for ourselves, for our authenticity. Many of our so-called deficiencies, vulnerability,

uncertainty, dependencies, low self-confidence and the like originate in the early childhood. They were caused by those who cared
for us who educated us, those who did not know better, who themselves got stuck in such behaviour patterns and got solidified in
them. Let's have the courage to find new paths, to dissolve old patterns and to free ourselves from gridlocked dogmas. Who, if not we,
brings an end to these rigid patterns, crystallised over the ages, having brought and still bringing so much inconvenience, war, suffering
and separation into the world. Who, if not we? When, if not now!

The most important thing is to ask myself: Am I in line with what
I am thinking, feeling, and doing? Am I close to my inner child? Does
it serve for my healing regarding physical and spiritual aspects? Do
I experience deep inner satisfaction or do I expect recognition, admi-
ration and love from the outside? What is the result of relations and
situations stealing only energy and substance, making us tired and
in the end speed up our aging process? Real anti-ageing for body,
mind and soul starts with the acceptance of the circumstances of our
live which we cannot change. What we can do is to make them part
of our life, release our resistances and it all ends up with clear and
conscious decisions for our lives, fulfilling them with all consequences and taking over the responsibility for them.

Being able to distinguish beneficial from inappropriate things is
a real challenging job. Easiness and happiness will be the following
result. We will be courageous, authentic and content and do no
longer have to search for appreciation and recognition for our ego
on the outside. If we reconcile with everyday circumstances, we gain
more clarity. If we heal old injuries of our soul (this is what we are
absolutely able to do) every one of us can do that, we gain more and
more consciousness of our self. We esteem and value our divine essence and are no longer willing to be manipulated by others or to
deny our true being in order to please others.

Every situation and relationship helps me to ripen if I am prepared to learn the lesson behind it, if I can accept the task and the challenge life is offering me. Thus, we become more and more conscious, dedicated people who are able to manage their lives and are totally aware of their original task of life. This is all part of the quality of the new era that has just begun, that wants to be experienced, that proceeds more and more and in which we play an important part.

Mercy, primarily for us, is the key to true and pure love. We cannot expect that our future will be nice and rosy unless we have properly cleared and cleaned our past. Only if we start seeing our life as a totally neutral and unbiased experience and are thankful for it, we are able to enter a conscious and happy creation of our future. This way, we are giving our life a new order.

"There are no coincidences; everything is according to these laws."

As the saying goes in the Kybalion:

Like a miracle, but only a simple principle of nature! Behind every occurrence there is a law. This law is often called Maya or the veil of illusionary perception of reality which we are unable to recognize. However, this does not mean that we have the right to deny its existence. Stones fell down on earth even at times when the law of falling bodies were not yet discovered.

3. The Law of Vibration

"Nothing rests; everything moves; everything vibrates."

The Kybalion

This is the principle that was already discovered by hermetic masters thousands of years ago and again appeared in Greek philosophy. Then, it fell into oblivion for a long time. In the course of the 19th century, modern sciences rediscovered this law. Since the 20th century, when sciences were celebrating their triumph, especially in the discovery of quantum physics, it has undoubtedly been proven and clear that everything is vibration. We now know that all matter is vibrating, even all thoughts and emotions, power, energy, electricity, magnetism, all these appearances manifest vibrations, only to be distinguished by different frequencies.

The slower something is vibrating the more solid it appears to our senses. Matter has the lowest/slowest vibration. It is the form of existence that has manifested the farthest from its source, the All/the origin, which is why it seems solid to us. The higher something is vibrating, the further it will proceed into its divine source, towards the All and the more it is made of fine and high vibration. This is also the principle based on which the various levels are divided into according to the law of correspondence.

In 1908 the three initiates describe the similarity and the differences of views concerning this topic in hermetic philosophy and modern sciences as follows:

"In the first place, science teaches that all matter manifests, in some degree, the vibrations arising from temperature or heat. Be an object cold or hot – both being but degrees of the same things – it manifests certain heat vibrations, and in that sense is in motion and vibration. Then all particles of Matter are in circular movement, from corpuscle to suns. The planets revolve around suns, and many of them turn on their axes. The suns move around greater central points, and these are believed to move around still greater, and so on, ad infinitum. The molecules of which the

particular kinds of Matter are composed are in a state of constant vibration and movement around each other and against each other. The molecules are composed of Atoms, which, likewise, are in a state of constant
movement and vibration. The atoms are composed of Corpuscles, sometimes called "electrons," "ions," etc., which also are in a state of rapid motion, revolving around each other, and which manifest a very rapid state
and mode of vibration. And, so we see that all forms of Matter manifest
Vibration, in accordance with the Hermetic Principle of Vibration.

And so it is with the various forms of Energy. Science teaches that
Light, Heat, Magnetism and Electricity are but forms of vibratory motion
connected in some way with, and probably emanating from the Ether. Science does not as yet attempt to explain the nature of the phenomena
known as Cohesion, which is the principle of Molecular Attraction; nor
Chemical Affinity, which is the principle of Atomic Attraction; nor Gravi-
tation (the greatest mystery of the three), which is the principle of attraction by which every particle or mass of Matter is bound to every other
particle or mass. These three forms of Energy are not as yet understood by
science, yet the writers incline to the opinion that these too are manifestations of some form of vibratory energy, a fact which the Hermetists have
held and taught for ages past.

The Universal Ether, which is postulated by science without its nature being understood clearly, is held by the Hermetists to be but a
higher manifestation of that which is erroneously called matter — that is
to say, Matter at a higher degree of vibration — and is called by them
"The Ethereal Substance." The Hermetists teach that this Ethereal Substance is of extreme tenuity and elasticity, and pervades universal space,
serving as a medium of transmission of waves of vibratory energy, such
as heat, light, electricity, magnetism, etc. The Teachings are that The
Ethereal Substance is a connecting link between the forms of vibratory
energy known as "Matter" on the one hand, and "Energy or Force" on
the other; and also that it manifests a degree of vibration, in rate and
mode, entirely its own."

In our daily life the principle of vibration is the main tool at our disposal for the practical use of the spiritual laws for our personal transformation. The Kybalion even says: He who understands the principle of vibration has gained the sceptre of power. Why is this principle that important according to the Kybalion? By means of the law of vibration, we are able to produce every desired condition of mind.

If we experience destructive emotions with low vibration, emotions dragging us and our surrounding down, as for example anger, jealousy or sadness, bringing a kind of heaviness to our life. It is possible to transform this condition into higher vibrating emotions like happiness, empathy, love, thankfulness, dedication and the like.

Nature always tends to strive to the higher vibration, i.e. towards its source. The naturally prescribed direction thus is the pole of the higher and faster vibration leading us from the deepest point of physical being into ever higher conditions and grades of vibration. We may take advantage here if we cooperate with the principle of vibration.

For a more precise understanding of this law there is a vivid illustration in the Kybalion which we want to explain here as exemplary: A wheel starts turning slowly. Our eyes recognise how the wheel is rotating; however, we do not perceive any sound or anything else. When the wheel starts rotating faster we notice a sound, a deep humming. When the wheel turns faster and faster we suddenly hear the single sounds of the musical scale up to the highest tone we are able to perceive with our sense of hearing. Our senses only work in a rather limited frequency thus only perceiving a limited part of reality. For this reason we theoretically only see a deep red when we do not hear any sound seeing the wheel rotating further and further. Following this idea of the wheel rotating faster and faster we see a colour spectrum of red, orange, yellow, green, blue, indigo blue up to violet.

Considering the object is rotating further, even faster, we become unable to see the colours because ultra violet cannot be seen with our eyes. Following are x-rays, the phenomenon of electricity and magnetism, all these areas which science explains to us.

Please note that this is a hypothetic experiment because perceiving x-rays means that atoms have already dissolved and the object has ceased to exist.

Scientific research blocks at this point because it is not willing to imagine what would happen if the hypothetic object were rotating further and at even higher speed. Hermetics go even beyond. After the object has dissolved into its ingredients and all atoms are decomposed, vibration may still increase following all areas of mental vibration. Here, the encounter of thoughts, feelings, all mental levels and spirituality take place. Even on the first levels of the mental area there is vibration and movement up to the highest level meaning that movement returns to its source. This way, evolution has found its determination and its aim in involution. The eternal circle in which universe after universe are created and exposed, recollects itself, returning to the eternal divine lap.

The famous mathematician Burkhard Heim has called this aspect, the All/God the 'unmoved mover'. It was also him who calculated reality from 12 different dimensions by finding a conclusion from obvious purely mathematic reasons. However, until today the best mathematicians in the world are still not able to understand his aspects of thinking. If they had understood, science would have been stepped one big step forward. Only the first four of these 12 mathematically calculable dimensions can be perceived with our senses:

length, width, height and time; and we think this is the entire reality, just because we are unable to perceive more with our limited senses.

The lower a vibration, the more it can be perceived and experienced by us and the easier can we learn about its existence. The higher a frequency of vibration the more it is invisible to and unperceivable for our senses. The level of vibration is decisive for our perception. The slower/lower the vibration, the more it is of rough material, the faster/higher the vibration, the more subtle it is.

In everyday life the parameter for checking our vibration is our mood because the two phenomena are directly linked to each other. We can perfectly imagine the low vibration if we are upset, in a bad mood or having negative feelings. Here, as human beings, we have to do with the vibration levels of our atoms, the levels of matter, dissolving further and further from solid matter into the higher levels of the mind. It is the task of our consciousness to refine and to spread until it is again aware of its origin and is able to lift itself up to the levels of the highest and pure mind. There, on the highest levels, there is the divine source, here, original ideas are born.

Christianity names these original ideas the arch angels; they represent certain basic strengths and ideas. The birth of a universe includes the idea of a certain experience; it is a common spiritual idea finding its shape. The shape means deceleration thus step-by-step creating the various levels of matter. Our universe comprises the idea of experience in the shape of trinity, i.e. the figure three. This is the special experience our universe is based upon. Just as we realise our ideas, first created in our brain, before they get their solid shape. Everybody who has ever been creative bringing his ideas into the world is able to comprehend and to confirm this procedure.

This is how we might imagine the process of creation by means of the law of correspondence even on the levels of pure mind where universes are created. The ability to try out at any time, creating new universes, is a process without beginning or end. However, for the human brain which is product of this process itself this is incomprehensible. All these ideas start vibrating as soon as they have been given a 'shape' thus becoming part of our material experience.

Regarding vibration the only thing we can rely on is the insight that everything is changing, nothing stands still, everything is in constant movement. There are planets in the universe that circle around each other, our sun circles around the next sun up to the central sun. We learn that the all is in constant movement, never stands still or comes to an end, as the ancient Greeks found out: 'Panta rhei – everything flows.' We too, are in constant movement: Like planets our thoughts circle around their own axis, producing even more new thoughts.

The law of vibration is a wonderful tool for us to work with in our daily life in order to have more control over our feelings and thoughts. We are able to make use of this principle if we wish to attract things which are useful for us by bringing ourselves on a new frequency of vibration, i.e. a level that allows us to consequently attract the desired object.

It is the same regularity: Just as a tuning fork is able to make differently tuned forks vibrate if they are on the same level of frequency, we will only be able to attract those experiences in our lives which are on the same frequency as our own thoughts, feelings and unconscious energies. If we allow negative emotions like jealousy, envy, anger, intolerance and fear to grow in us we activate the low vibrating tuning fork thus making experiences corresponding to exactly these emotions.

We thus enter a self-reinforcing circle because the negative experiences result in further negative thoughts and emotions leading to exactly the same negative experiences in our lives. This means that if we have negative experiences, we should encounter them with positive feelings and thoughts in order to disrupt the commencing vicious circle. This is why it is of utmost importance that we are always aware of our actual situation, gain insight in it and decide to choose a conscious inner reaction to it by increasing our vibrational level instead of unconsciously sticking to our negative thoughts and behaviour patterns.

Our vibrational level has a direct influence on our physical health. If we are vibrating rather low, we are vulnerable to colds, viruses and bacteria. We do not have strong consciousness of our body, for our surrounding and, even less, for our environment. The same applies to our nutrition: seasonal, light vegetarian food is much higher in vibration and thus much healthier than heavy, animal source, imported and industrially produced food. It is possible to bring ourselves into a higher cleaning and healing vibration by means of the right nutrition or by fasting cures, by conscious breathing and movement.

Even special music, dance, walks in nature, spiritual literature and mainly Yoga, Tai Chi and Qigong are wonderful, strengthening, meditative movements supporting us to come into a harmonious resonance with ourselves. All these are possibilities helping us to return to our middle and to remain there permanently. The higher vibration is always stronger than the lower vibration as this is the natural flow of nature.

If we understand how we can always increase our vibration good fortune will be with us. We finally become aware of the fact that nobody is responsible for our emotional life but we ourselves. We have the key in our hands and decide upon how to use it. We can use it for or against ourselves; this is up to our own decision...

4. The Law of Polarity

"Everything is dual; everything has poles; everything has its pair of opposites; like and unlike are the same; opposites are identical in nature, but different in degree; extremes meet; all truths are but half-truths; all paradoxes may be reconciled."

The Kybalion

The principle 'Everything is two-fold, everything has two poles.' is well known to us from nature. We find it in the polar manifestations of day and night, male and female, ebb and flow etc. The principle 'Counterparts are only identical regarding their nature' can be recognised with heat and cold. They are naturally not identical; the differences are only in the grades. The thermometer shows many grades, the lowest pole is called 'cold' the highest is called 'hot'. Between these two poles there are many grades between 'heat' and 'cold'. The higher of two grades is always 'warmer' while the lower one is always 'colder'.

There is no absolute measurement; everything is depending on the grade. There is no point on the thermometer, where heat stops and cold starts. This is the naturally given polarity in which our material being is embedded in. As explained with the aforementioned principles, the vibration principle does also play an important role for the principle of polarity because vibration is only possible between two poles. If there were only one pole, there would neither be movement nor our material world including our material body. Solid matter is based upon the principle of polarity.

Polarity caused by the aforementioned laws in our everyday views and attitudes is fatally equated with duality. We must clearly distinguish between polarity and duality. Polarity is a principle given by nature while duality is a totally artificial creation of the human mind. In duality we distinguish between good and bad, evaluating everything according to our personal human standards.

Naturally thinking, the positive and the negative are polar contradictions not claiming that one aspect were good and the other one bad. This evaluating differentiation has been formed by our dualistic view of the world. It is exactly this restricting dualistic view which has to disappear if we as individuals and as mankind wish to make clear progress, if we want to reach a higher level of consciousness. As long as we remain in our evaluating consciousness neatly separating everything into good and bad, there is no further development for us human beings. We will still be creators of separation, hatred and war. This is the way we will experience the results of our unfortunate dual views until we finally, through the pain and the suffering they bring us, start to gain insight.

As long as the vibration of separation and fear is in us, dual separating evaluation will be alive in us and we will not be able to be free. Those events we think are bad are as useful and instructive as the so-called good ones. Moreover, it is mostly much more useful because it shows us where our dark unconscious spaces are in our innermost and because it normally provokes thought.

Natural polarity is also located in our character because not all is equal, contrary to what some spiritual circles try to teach us. There are natural differences between the strong and the weak, however, they are totally free from evaluation. The stronger is not always the better, the weaker not always the worse. This may lead to a different handling of weaknesses and a clear view on them. These differences are alright and, therefore, they are important for our experiences and the resulting insights.

But, we read further in the Kybalion: 'Equal and unequal are the same.' What does this mean to us? How can we make use of this phenomenon in our everyday life? Let us for example look at our (ever changing) mood. If, for example, we feel scared in some situations, we may imagine a scale ranging from fear to courage: fear is the lowest and courage the highest level. By means of mental transmutation we are willingly able to shift our vibration, and thus our mood, towards courage or towards fear like with an inner regulator.

When we consciously influence our mood we apply the law of polarity: We decide upon which pole we wish to shift to and we apply the law of vibration because we change one vibration into another. We can do this with all our emotions and conditions of consciousness, in every situation we may decide to feel love or fear, plenitude or deficiency. We can imagine this procedure like a mixing desk. We push the regulator and thus not only our inner feeling but also the frequency we send to our surrounding immediately changes. This way we are paving the way to receive what we desire.

Commenting on this, the three initiates write in their book:

"The student who is familiar with the processes by which the various schools of Mental Science, etc., produce changes in the mental states of those following their teachings, may not readily understand the principle underlying many of these changes. When, however, the Principle of Polarity is once grasped, and it is seen that the mental changes are occasioned by a change of polarity – a sliding along the same scale – the matter is more readily understood. The change is not in the nature of a transmutation of one thing into another thing entirely different – but is

merely a change of degree in the same things, a vastly important difference."

Conscious differentiation of polarity and duality is the one and only principle of peace. It is even the biggest one because it may lead to a general recciliation of the poles we experience as contradictions. Due to our missing distinction and constant confusion of polarity and duality we have begun to separate natural polarity into good and bad. Making this principle aware for ourselves and working with the law we find out that the so-called contradictions of nature are identical, however, they differ by grade. They merge; there is no separation as it has been created by the dualistic view of the human beings.

As material beings the two poles are constantly in us. If we have one, we have the same potential of the other one in us: Where there is light, there is shadow. He who has fear has the same amount of courage. Fear can be seen as the inactive potential of courage which can be transformed into courage by means of mental transformation. Deficiency is the inactive potential of plenitude in us. This list could be continued endlessly.

Let us then start activating the mixing desk of our emotions, moods and attitudes regarding ourselves and our environment and shift the regulators in the direction which is useful and optimal for our purposes. Thus, we will become powerful creators of our own reality in all areas of our life, in health, fortune, relations, friendships and love.

If it is applied in the right manner, this law is a true gift for mankind because knowing how to apply it means to avoid every dispute. Where there is no dispute, no strife in our small lives, there will be no war in the big life because war starts in our minds. It begins so small and hidden with the first small dualistic point of view. Basically it is all about who is right and who is wrong and how to push through my own individual opinion which I think is the right one.

When we recognize that both poles have their right of existence and validity we begin to understand that every truth is only half the truth. No person is ever totally right and no one can be totally wrong. It always depends on the point of view we are assuming. I normally assume I am right with my opinion because I can only see it from my point of view. A simple shift of perspective would be enough to give my fellow human being the right to have a different point of view thus discovering that we are both right: Everyone is half way right and half way wrong. Then there will be no more reason for dispute and fight, at least no time for warfare.

The law of polarity can be understood and used as a universal principle of conciliation. When I have finally found out that I am principally only half way right as my counterpart is, there is no necessity to prevail my own opinion. I now understand the senselessness of this effort and I am now aiming at the integration of different points of view leading to a view of the world which appreciates the variety of facets of reality. This is more important than a unique implementation of a momentary single meaning although it is my own.

From a world of duality and separation we are reaching out to a world of harmony and unity. Our life will be much brighter, more interesting and vivid. My counterpart is no longer my enemy or my opponent because I see the individual soul delivering her very personal share within the big play of our world theatre. I am happy with her beauty, supporting her to tribute her share to enrich all beings in the world.

5. The Law of Rhythm

"Everything flows out and in; everything has its tides; all things rise and fall; the pendulum-swing manifests in everything; the measure of the swing to the right, is the measure of the swing to the left; rhythm compensates."

The Kybalion

The big hermetic principle of rhythm is closely connected with the law of polarity. Rhythm must be seen in conjunction with the law of polarity. Rhythm manifests between the two poles which have been established by the principle of polarity. The impetus of the pendulum always changes from one side to the other. The law of rhythm teaches us that everything in our world is subject to constant ascent and descent, from blooming to dying, from being born and to - dying. There is always movement from one pole to the other in an even rhythm. The strength of the impact of the pendulum to one side is according to the strength of the impact to the other side. This rule is observed in every creation in nature - from the rhythmic circle of atoms and molecules as in the creation and vanishing of sun systems and universes.

Every being manifests in action and reaction, progress and regress, ascending and sinking. All living systems, plants, animals and human beings are subject to the rhythm of birth, growing, ripening, decline, death and then again: a new birth. This can even be observed in our systems, in the creation and destroying of nations, cultures, philosophies, conventions, customs and confessions of faith. Everything that has come into being will begin the process of deterioration on the height of its power. There is no standstill, no absolute silence, no interruption of movement; all movement is subject to the law of rhythm. There is the ongoing and eternal 'inhaling and exhaling of Brahman', as the Vedes describe it metaphorically.

This means that 'being over the moon' is undoubtedly followed by 'down to the dumps'. If we accept this rule we know that we cannot always be 'over the moon', i.e. that it is only natural that the pendulum goes to the other side. However, the principle of rhythm can be neutralised with regard to its influence on our mood: We can stop being dragged along emotionally when the pendulum goes to the other side because we know that this is only the natural compensation which we do not necessarily have to follow like sheep has when driven to the slaughter. By mentally concentrating on the positive pole and not having our consciousness influenced by the swing of the pendulum towards the other pole, we are no longer helplessly exposed to the daily events and situations. We become more balanced, more constant and are literally standing above it all. We will thus become conscious co-creators of nature, taking our sensitivities, our vibration and thus our fate in our own hands.

Swinging back of the pendulum is called the law of compensation which means that everything will be compensated. Day is followed by night, richness is followed by poorness and happiness is followed by grief. This does not necessarily take place within one life; it may expand over several incarnations. It is the natural flow of life and it is good because it tributes to our experience thus giving our soul maturity. Suffering always is the result of our personal valuation. Richness is good, poverty is bad. Is it really like that? If we are able to release this dual view of the world there will be no more reason for suffering.

Rich or poor, big or small, everything is fine as it is, everything is of divine origin. We now comprehend that suffering is something artificially created by our brain and is of no use to us. Thus, our small ego sometimes wants to be comforted because it is not able to let go and wants to show its power to the surrounding in some situations. If we are able to let go during the most demanding phases of our lives, if we accept situations and find out about their meaning for us, we can perfectly take advantage of these experiences for our progress.

Our dual view of the world is often expressed by means of extreme either-or behaviour which is an exclusiveness followed by separation and separating us from our fellow beings and from our own wholeness. If we succeed in aiming our consciousness on a both...and...-approach where one supplements the other, we will be able to return to our natural wholeness on an individual basis and society as a whole; like Yin and Yang are forming a wholeness, because one is not possible without the other. There is no day without night, no ebb without flood. They are serving each other. This way, we learn to deal with the ascending and descending powers of nature, making them serve us. We learn that inconvenient things are as useful as convenient ones. We will be able to create new attitudes of thinking which are beyond all dualistic comprehension because we understand that dual thinking and acting is now useless because we are in need of new mental concepts.

We should be able to reach a condition in which we are no longer depending on the forces acting in and around us. This can be achieved if we distinct ourselves energetically from the moods of our fellow beings and not let them have an influence on our well-being. Our true inner stability can be determined by external influences. The more we reach a fixed and unshakeable stability the less we are helplessly exposed to the outside, thus becoming stronger and more stable. It takes long until we become solid as a rock and no more helpless like a piece of driftwood on the ocean of life.

The three initiates write on this topic:

"The Principle of Rhythm is well understood by modern science, and is considered a universal law as applied to material things. But the Hermetists carry the principle much further, and know that its manifestations and influence extend to the mental activities of Man, and that it accounts for the bewildering succession of moods, feelings and other annoying and

perplexing changes that we notice in ourselves. But the Hermetists by studying the operations of this Principle have learned to escape some of its activities by Transmutation.

The Hermetic Masters long since discovered that while the Principle of Rhythm was invariable, and ever in evidence in mental phenomena, still there were two planes of its manifestation so far as mental phenomena are concerned. They discovered that there were two general planes of Consciousness, the Lower and the Higher, the understanding of which fact enabled them to rise to the higher plane and thus escape the swing of the Rhythmic pendulum which manifested on the lower plane. In other words, the swing of the pendulum occurred on the Unconscious Plane, and the Consciousness was not affected."

We will come back to this topic in more detail in the next chapter by discussing the law of neutralisation and we will see that it is of fundamental importance for the development of an enlarged consciousness.

6. The Law of Cause and Effect

"Every Cause has its Effect; every Effect has its Cause; everything happens according to Law; Chance is but a name for Law not recognized; there are many planes of causation, but nothing escapes the Law."

The Kybalion

The sixth hermetic principle is the great principle of order in our universe saying that there is no coincidence at all. Such coincidence would not be reasonable within the order of our universe because here, basically nothing can happen by coincidence. There is no space for coincidence in such a highly well-organised system like our universe because if it was, the whole structure would then break down and end up in unholy confusion. If for example the moon would start rotating around the world in opposite direction or the sun would stop shining for a few days, even the smallest of change in any of nature's parameters, would set an abrupt end to life on earth, purely by coincidence...

The old hermetic philosophers state that the term 'coincidence' is only an expression for the fact that we are still unable to see the reason behind it. As we have learned from the aforementioned laws, phenomena of life are continuing. Without interruption and without exception they follow the laws, the rise and the fall, the polar contradictions, the vibration and the correspondence of all levels of being.

The first law already unmasks the legend of coincidence. From where should it come if it wasn't part of the big play, if it wasn't born from the mind of the All itself? We have already understood that there is nothing outside the All because otherwise it would not be the All. Being thus preserved in the mind of the All it is dependent on its rules and cannot place itself outside.

The principle of cause and effect is also basis of all scientific thinking. Although quantum physicists claim there are things in the quantum world which happen purely by coincidence we may assume the fact that this discipline is rather young and has researched very little and, therefore, the reasons are out of reach for us and may be only recognised by future generation scientists.

In the book of the three initiates the illusion of the idea of 'coincidence' is explained by means of a good example:

"The word Chance is derived from a word meaning "to fall" (as the falling of dice), the idea being that the fall of the dice (and many other happenings) are merely a "happening" unrelated to any cause. And this is the sense in which the term is generally employed. But when the matter is closely examined, it is seen that there is no chance whatsoever about the fall of the dice. Each time a die falls, and displays a certain number, it

obeys a law as infallible as that which governs the revolution of the plan-
ets around the sun. Back of the fall of the die are causes, or chains of
causes, running back further than the mind can follow. The position of the
die in the box; the amount of muscular energy expended in the throw; the
condition of the table, etc., etc., all are causes, the effect of which may be
seen. But back of these seen causes there are chains of unseen preceding
causes, all of which had a bearing upon the number of the die which fell
uppermost.

If a die be cast a great number of times, it will be found that the num-
bers shown will be about equal, that is, there will be an equal number of
one-spot, two-spot, etc., coming uppermost. Toss a penny in the air, and
it may come down either "heads" or "tails"; but make a sufficient num-
ber of tosses, and the heads and tails will about even up. This is the oper-
ation of the law of average. But both the average and the single toss come
under the Law of Cause and Effect, and if we were able to examine into
the preceding causes, it would be clearly seen that it was simply impossi-
ble for the die to fall other than it did, under the same circumstances and
at the same time. Given the same causes, the same results will follow.
There is always a "cause" and a "because" to every event. Nothing ever
"happens" without a cause, or rather a chain of causes."

The law of cause and effect, as it is called, is of great importance
as it shows us that everything in life we encounter is the result of a
preceding reason. If all being, every experience, every life situation
- even every thought - is only the result of a reason that already took
place long before, it means, vice versa, that we are able to create desired effects by consciously setting reasons bringing the requested
results in future. By means of this law we really become creators of
our own reality, create exactly those experiences and situations we
wish to have in life and we are no longer playthings of external powers.

This principle makes us understand that there is no coincidence. No event, no stroke of faith, nothing that would not be in our responsibility. Nothing that would not be the result of an action we did before. Be it that we unconsciously put energy in it, denying our creative potential thus making ourselves passive playthings for the surrounding forces. As long as we do not understand this principle are we playthings of reasons other human beings are responsible for. This principle allows us to create every reality desired thus eliminating any fear of serious strokes of fate.

Our entire universe is basing on the fact that every event has its reason in a preceding thus leading to a further event according to the rules. We are embedded in a sea of cause-and-action relations. No event 'creates' sui generis another event; however, it is only one link in a large chain of events coming from the creative energy of the all. Hence there is an uninterrupted causal relationship between all occurrences since time immemorial and far beyond, since the creation of the universe. All things are in relation to cause-and-action in which we actively participate in. We can consciously make use of this knowledge or remain in the passive role of play figures. It is always up to our personal decision to be a powerful creator or a poor 'victim', just as we like it.

For sure, it happens hardly by coincidence that these universal laws are being revealed now - in the transition time between the Age of Pisces and the Age of Aquarius, thus reaching a larger number of people. While the Age of Pisces first and foremost meant manipulation and abuse of power that are now finally coming to an end, the quality of the Age of Aquarius is characterised by the fact that every human being can become a master/creator. Again, we are learning that everything has its proper order; everything happens at the right time...

When time for change has come the necessary resources and knowledge will be available for us. It is up to us to take them and to restrain from other-directed behaviour of victims by reaching self-determined causality thinking. No more passive and wrong obedience to our surrounding and the wishes of others, however, not allowing ourselves to drift because of our moods and atmospheres. There is no more need for us to be restricted by early childhood embossments, even not by our genetic determinations in whatever way and, in case of failure, making easy excuses because of them.

The laws introduced here reveal rules of life that can bring us into contact with our highest power. They give us advice how to manage our own moods, character and attitudes. Now it is our turn to use them accordingly or to decide to be play pieces on the board games of others who are using these laws for their advantage, pushing us around all the time. It is now up to us to decide for every single moment in time whether we wish to be players in the big play of life, actively setting reasons or if we want to passively suffer from the results. If we want to walk this way of arbitrariness, of creativity, this means that we foremost want to clear our mind, abandoning time-honoured opinions and convictions by clear distinction, sharp minded and with alert consciousness, realizing the new quality of human existence.

Although we do not discuss the topic 'free will' or 'pre-determination' in this book (we will come back to that issue in the following book) I have to admit that the more conscious we already are, the more perfect we can use our free will. The less conscious we are, the more we remain stuck in material, dual consciousness and the smaller our possibility for the use of our free will becomes. Like the old sayings expressly say: 'The further the creation is away from its centre point the more it is bound; the more it approaches its centre, the freer it is.'

Approving the cause-and-action principle we also may move away from the idea of 'guilt' which has now become obsolete. As we may conclude from this law there is no guilt at all. It is an invention of the human brain. If everything results from cause and action where should be the idea of guilt? There is a cause and an action resulting thereof, but there is no guilt. Although this attitude meanwhile has become good habit it is not right to blame someone or some external circumstances for the own failure. This mainly has to do with laziness and rejection of self-responsibility. The results we reject in such moments because it is easier to make complaints to others are those we must be responsible for because we have drawn them into our lives. If we are honest with ourselves and critically regarding our actions of the past, we will learn about the reasons we set ourselves.

However, it would be unreasonable to react with blaming oneself. It was our decision because we did/could not know better and we will learn from these experiences, willing to find further development and acting in a more healing way for us and our environment. A basic requirement for an affectionate and attentive encounter of human beings is the ability to forgive ourselves, to accept us as we are on all levels, physically and mentally, with dignity in the sense of our higher self/our essence, loving us.

The law of cause and action is the basis of the karma principle forming the basis of all big spiritual traditions. The law of karma (also refer to chapter 3) says that there is repetition of patterns and processes over several lives until we have learned the lessons behind and have released the life-restricting programming of our consciousness. However, it is not about finding guilt which is an illusion as we all know. It is about getting rid of all structures of thinking and patterns of behaviour which are not useful for us. Contrary to our ancestors we now have the necessary knowledge and means to carry out our own transformation. There is no excuse any more not to take control of our life. Let us again become conscious, self-responsible observers and co-creators of our existence! Let us face the fact that the reactions we now see were caused by ourselves yesterday (or even in a previous life)!

The crucial point determining our karma is unintentional action because the action behind our actions and decisions determines the following reaction. It is thus not the action itself that is determining on the result. Unintentional action means to escape from the wheel of karma. Even 'good' intentions result in karma because **my** well-meant recommendations and actions are based on **my** restricted individual point of view and may possibly not be good for other persons. A thing being good for one person may even be totally inappropriate for another one. We can often see that proven regarding well-meant advices or educational measures taken by parents with regard to their children. I want, I mean, I just want to... all this is only coming from our ego consciousness providing old programmes, basing on control obsession, deficiency of consciousness or any other fear.

Action based on that fundament will no longer be able to make us happy and not be able to give us peace in the long term. Every intention includes expectation behind it. This expectation causes stress and costs us a lot of energy. Although it may be a long way to achieve really unintentional acting without any expectations, simply free of validation, however, it is worth going it. In a totally new way it may help us become free and relaxed. Even the intention is the result of our will.

If my actions are determined by my divine will instead of the will of my ego the decisive factor is wholeness. This means that I release an idea or a condition I am longing for and trust that the right things will happen to me. I do not have any expectation regarding a certain outcome of the action. This also implies that there will not be any disappointment for me due to expectations which have not been fulfilled.

The deep, real desire of the heart without firm expectation may persist; the small ego-wish must die; otherwise, we will never be free. I am doing what I have to do according to the best of my knowledge and belief and then, I let go. I will always do my best, however, without expectation. As soon as something is connected with pressure and constraint, there is no longer unintentional action and I am bound to the wheel of karma.

When I start trusting, the right things will absolutely happen to me right on time. A new awareness of life may arise, unexpected confidence, easiness, freedom and happiness, a liveliness that would not be able to find its place within our fearful small ego-consciousness. The knowledge necessary for this step is offered to us in the spiritual laws; now it is only up to us to make use of them.

7. The Law of Gender

"Gender is in everything; everything has its Masculine and Feminine Principles; Gender manifests on all planes."

The Kybalion

The principle of gender says that there is gender on every level of being, male and female are the basis of all being. Here, the word 'gender' is meant in its general meaning and not as an expression of gender which only aims at the physical differences between male and female beings.

The mission of the male principle, in Yoga literature also called the principle of consciousness, seems to be to start the process of creation by giving the female principle a certain amount of energy during a conscious act. The female principle, in Yoga called 'Shakti', the principle of energy/power is the one accomplishing the active creative process. Thus, both need and determine each other as it is beautifully illustrated in the symbol of Yin and Yang. Without assistance, none of them would be able to create something new. Even if both principles are united in one organism the law behind them is always acting.

Science has not yet managed to accept this principle behind all levels of being. However, there is clear evidence that in the creation of crystals there is something that seems to correspond to the hermetic law of gender. In the field of energy, power and electricity, at the source of their manifestation, there is also clear evidence for the presence of gender and its activities. Regarding the scientific provability of this principle, the three initiates even go one step beyond, saying:

"The latest scientific teachings are that the creative corpuscles or electrons are Feminine (science says "they are composed of negative electricity" – we say they are composed of Feminine energy). A Feminine corpuscle becomes detached from, or rather leaves, a Masculine corpuscle, and starts on a new career. It actively seeks a union with a Masculine corpuscle, being urged thereto by the natural impulse to create new forms of Matter or Energy. One writer goes so far as to use the term "it at once seeks, of its own volition, a union," etc. This detachment and uniting form the basis of the greater part of the activities of the chemical world. When the Feminine corpuscle unites with a Masculine corpuscle, a certain process is begun. The Feminine particles vibrate rapidly under the influence of the Masculine energy, and circle rapidly around the latter. The result is the birth of a new atom.

This new atom is really composed of a union of the Masculine and Feminine electrons, or corpuscles, but when the union is formed the atom is a separate thing, having certain properties, but no longer manifesting the property of free electricity. The process of detachment or separation of the Feminine electrons is called "ionization." These electrons, or corpuscles, are the most active workers in Nature's field. Arising from their unions, or combinations, manifest the varied phenomena of light, heat, electricity, magnetism, attraction, repulsion, chemical affinity and the reverse, and similar phenomena. And all this arises from the operation of the Principle of Gender on the plane of Energy. (...)"

Mental Gender

In the field of spirituality the male principle corresponds to the objective, active, conscious, giving, positive, warm, expanding, quick, dry, bright, etc. The female principle comprises the subjective, passive, unconscious, negative, cold, contracting, slow, moist, dark.

Focussing our view to the inside, towards our self-perception we are able to perceive the principle of Mental Gender. The first thing we are encountering is the perception of 'I am'. Further examination reveals that this perception is separated in two parts: in an 'I' and a 'Me'. The 'Me' we are normally fatally calling 'I' is determined by our emotions, sympathy, antipathy, habits, characteristic features, etc. that altogether make up our normal personality. We know that these emotions and feelings change, that they are subject to the principle of rhythm and polarity. This is the part of us we usually identify with our normal ego-consciousness and think it is our true being, resulting in all those sinister consequences already discussed.

Persistent and serious self-surveillance can help us gain higher consciousness, loosening our identification with our 'Me', our ego. Directing our view further to the inside we find out that this inner dimension cannot be our true being, our essence because it can be changed according to the demands. As a result, there must be an instance in us causing this change. This dimension can then be called our true 'ego', our core being, the point in us from which we are able to change our thoughts, our feelings and even our consciousness which, however, remain unchanged themselves. These two levels in us realise the hermetic principle of gender.

The 'Me' with the potential to create descendants in the form of thoughts, ideas, feelings and other mental conditions may regarded here as the female principle, as Shakti, which must obtain a conscious impulse as a kind of energy from the male principle the 'ego' (its own or the 'ego' of another person) in order to be able to form its own mental creations. This procedure is the basis of all creative power.

Here, the 'ego' is the level of consciousness which is able to allow the 'Me' to work according to certain creative rules thus being able to witness the mental process of creation quasi from the outside. It represents the aspect of 'being' contrary to the 'Me' which is the aspect of 'becoming'.

The three initiates write on the application of the principle of mental gender in daily life:

"The strong men and women of the world invariably manifest the Masculine Principle of Will, and their strength depends materially upon this fact. Instead of living upon the impressions made upon their minds by others, they dominate their own minds by their Will, obtaining the kind of

mental images desired, and moreover dominate the minds of others likewise, in the same manner. Look at the strong people, how they manage to implant their seed-thoughts in the minds of the masses of the people, thus causing the latter to think thoughts in accordance with the desires and wills of the strong individuals. This is why the masses of people are such sheep-like creatures, never originating an idea of their own, nor using their own powers of mental activity.

The manifestation of Mental Gender may be noticed all around us in everyday life. The magnetic persons are those who are able to use the Masculine Principle in the way of impressing their ideas upon others. The actor who makes people weep or cry as he wills, is employing this principle. And so is the successful orator, statesman, preacher, writer or other people who are before the public attention. The peculiar influence exerted by some people over others is due to the manifestation of Mental Gender, along the Vibratorial lines above indicated. In this principle lies the secret of personal magnetism, personal influence, fascination, etc., as well as the phenomena generally grouped under the name of Hypnotism."

WAY OF THE HEART

Introduction

The seven spiritual laws described in the previous chapters form the part which until today –has been known from the Kybalion, the heart piece of the Tabula Smaragdina of hermetic philosophy. As already mentioned, this knowledge was kept strictly secret over the centuries and was only orally transmitted from the master to the pupil initiated. It was only in 1908 that the first writing on the Kybalion was published by the three initiates, who, due to the above-mentioned reasons of secrecy, did not reveal their true identities at that time. In this book they described the seven spiritual laws all phenomena of life are subjected to. Those seven laws form the basis of all big religions and spiritual traditions of our world.

Nothing can be found in any of the world religions that would not have its origin in these few laws, of course much more decorated with numerous metaphors, illustrations and stories in order to give the people of the corresponding time access and to help them integrate the rules in their everyday lives. Of course, much of the knowledge has also been blurred, especially as soon as religions were institutionalised and degenerated as instruments of power of the elite. We have to admit now that it is a great gift for mankind that this original knowledge in its pure and unchanged nature is accessible which is the common source of all religions; by uniting them they terminate every struggle and disharmony between them. Thus, we are now able to clearly acknowledge that they basically all claim the same wisdom, taken from the one and only source.

Coming across this wisdom I found out that it is all about the so-called 'philosopher's stone', the missing link which not only reconciles the religions, but also the two big paths of insight: science and spirituality. I started studying these principles and did research until I became aware of the fact that besides these seven there are two further laws which, however, shall only be revealed if it is time for them, i.e. if mankind has developed enough mental maturity to understand them. This time has now come: At the beginning of the Age of Aquarius the complete 'esoteric' meaning (secret) knowledge of the world shall be revealed and made public so that everybody who wishes to do so, would be able to walk the path of enlightenment, gaining mastership in his own manner without any Gurus, spiritual masters or other (self-appointed) mediators between 'God' and mankind.

Upon intensive study of the hermetic teachings these two laws can certainly be closed although they are mentioned here and there in another context. Hence, they were not yet expressively mentioned among the basic principles which built the universe. This will be the task of this book and I am doing my best to meet these high expectations. Please apologize if I should fail in this first effort, I will write more on this topic in the following years to the extent that this knowledge will be revealed to me more and more.

Additionally to the two missing principles (the 8th and the 9th law) I will make a small change in the sequence of the laws which - in my opinion - were deliberately interchanged in their first publication 1908 in order to maintain a certain degree of disguise of the truth. Due to this change and the addition of the 8th and 9th law we suddenly realised that there is a most beautiful description of a whole cycle of creation. It is an illustration of the path from pure mental aspect/from 'God' into matter ('becoming flesh'/incarnation) and back to god, back to unity/to the original condition of being.

We now know why these two laws and the right chronological order are only to be revealed now. It is because now time has come that it will be possible for all human beings and not only some selected initiates, Yogis, monks or other spiritual masters to walk the path of enlightenment/path of awaking, the path back to God.

The Keystone of the Pyramid

The lost keystone of the pyramid is a key to the hidden wisdom the secret builder of the pyramid is said to have hidden because of the coming flood, so that it would last forever and become visible in due time.

'*Following the report of the Arabic historian al-Makrizi (1364 - 1442 AD) an Egyptian king named Saurîd started 300 years before the (biblical) flood the building of the pyramids of Gizeh in order to safeguard the complete knowledge of that time and to save it from the catastrophe. On top of the big pyramid (Cheops), on the keystone, there was a scripture showing who the builder was, when it was built and that it was completed within six years. The reference to king Saurîd is of great interest here because according to the 33rd chapter of Hitat he would be identical with the Hebrew Henoch, the Greek Hermes Trismegistos and also the Egyptian king Saurîd. The Hitat is the historical work of al-Makrizi.*'

From: 'The order of the prophet Henoch'

The key stone of the pyramid thus symbolises the missing link, the two missing laws representing the knowledge on the entire circle of creation together with the seven known laws.

8. The Law of Neutralisation

'The connection of the two polar oppositions in the zero point leads to the overcoming of separation, paving the way back to unity.'

WAY OF THE HEART

Overcoming duality I release my karma, the eternal game of polarity. The only necessity is to stop dividing into good and bad, to stop valuating and to gain insight into myself. It is important to accept all my positive and negative points. Salvation of my shadows is done by accepting the own 'perpetration'. Thus, I proceed from being a victim towards the divine creative power. Neutralisation makes it possible to overcome the narrow boundaries of ego-consciousness in order to merge with the higher self in the material substance. This is the prerequisite to access the highest of laws.

With the seventh law, the principle of gender, the process of reunification of Shakti with Shiva began, to describe it with the metaphor from Yoga-philosophy. The separation, which started in the second law, the principle of correspondence (discussed in more detail at the end of the sixth chapter in the description of the WAY OF THE HEART), is now neutralised, the circuit is closed again. We start freeing ourselves from matter by overcoming of what we define as matter: polarity. The decisive feature of matter, explicitly described under the relevant laws of the preceding chapter, is the polarity of plus and minus, of the male and the female pole. Without polarity there would be no matter which, in the hermetic sense, is not only firm matter but also thoughts, emotions and all invisible forms of physical power, energy, magnetism etc.

If we want to make our way out of polarity, back into the (divine) unity we must of course overcome polarity. But how can this be achieved practically? I already mentioned the starting point; it is the 'sexual' act of unification of the male and the female pole. However, it has to be mentioned that here, 'sexual' is meant in its general meaning because the unification of a male and a female body is only a special form of the deeper meaning of the principle.

At this point we suddenly understand why the process of creation is really a creative one, why it aims in a certain direction and why the All expands more and more. New creation happens exactly where we make our way back to the divine home thus creating new 'life'. This way, the so-called circle of creation expands to a spiral of creation because the next cycle does not start at the same point but on the next level. The reason for this is the fact that new creation coming from unification (we may call it the new-born) bears the experience of the preceding cycle of creation thus forming the starting point for its own process of creation.

The direction of evolution, the eternal proceeding and advancement of creation can also be explained this way. Because in reality it is a spiral, not a circle, the image of the circle only comes up if we look on the spiral observing the eternally revolving circle of birth, growing, vanishing, dying and rebirth. If we change our point of view or the geometrical representation in the three-dimensional space, we see the shape of the spiral which is an ancient holy symbol of all cultures - a symbol of creation.

Let us now dare the next step from the principle of gender, from polarity back to unity, transcending the concept of the male and the female pole thus forming a balance which is the centre point between the two poles. As long as we tend to one or the other direction, male or female, we maintain energy and neutralisation will not be able. The same process takes place in chemistry; if we want to create a neutral substance from acid, we have to add as much alkaline solution that a stoichiometric exact balance is given. Unless we have discovered exactly the middle between plus and minus which is movement being an important feature of matter and resulting from the law of rhythm, we cannot come to a standstill and bring rest which is a prerequisite for our venture, the return to unity. The most characteristic feature of unity is quietness, total standstill; there is no more movement because the two poles causing movement have disappeared.

As a symbol for the law of gender TAO can be named where the curved line stands for movement. There, polarity still exists, but although in the symbol the core of the counter pole is present in the core of the other, it is already transcending. In connection with the principle of neutralisation we may also consider the symbol of two halves of a circle. There is no more movement, we are centred in the middle, both polar oppositions have already adapted; there is no more (coloured) differentiation, however, they can still be distinguished as the two halves of one thing.

The principle of neutralisation of course was discovered by the hermetic masters long time ago, but it has never before been described as an individual law, especially not as one that may help to find the way back into unity. Within the Kybalion it is only mentioned as a possibility to neutralise the reactions on the law of rhythm, in order to avoid the swinging of the pendulum to the 'negative' side. This is described in the following text of the book of the three initiates:

"The Hermetic Masters long since discovered that while the Principle of Rhythm was invariable, and ever in evidence in mental phenomena, still there were two planes of its manifestation so far as mental phenomena are concerned. They discovered that there were two general planes of

Consciousness, the Lower and the Higher, the understanding of which fact enabled them to rise to the higher plane and thus escape the swing of the Rhythmic pendulum which manifested on the lower plane. In other words, the swing of the pendulum occurred on the Unconscious Plane, and the Consciousness was not affected. This they call the Law of Neutralization.

Its operations consist in the raising of the Ego above the vibrations of the Unconscious Plane of mental activity, so that the negative-swing of the pendulum is not manifested in consciousness, and therefore they are not affected. It is akin to rising above a thing and letting it pass beneath you. The Hermetic Master, or advanced student, polarizes himself at the desired pole, and by a process akin to "refusing" to participate in the backward swing, or, if you prefer, a "denial" of its influence over him, he stands firm in his polarized position, and allows the mental pendulum to swing back along the unconscious plane.

All individuals who have attained any degree of self-mastery, accomplish this, more or less unknowingly, and by refusing to allow their moods and negative mental states to affect them, they apply the Law of Neutralization. The Master, however, carries this to a much higher degree of proficiency, and by the use of his Will he attains a degree of Poise and Mental Firmness almost impossible of belief on the part of those who allow themselves to be swung backward and forward by the mental pendulum of moods and feelings."

The picture of the pendulum in the above-mentioned text from the hermetic teachings also shows us a path to the creation of a neutral mind, how to balance the natural rhythmic swinging of pendulum of the polar material level willing to carry us to the other (undesired) pole. Here two possibilities can be defined:

We fixate spiritually, as the Hermetics call it, on the side of the desired pole having the pendulum swung beneath us to the other side, thus denying the effects the undesired pole has on our mood. In this situation of applied neutralisation the swing of the pendulum is not released totally because it still happens according to the law of rhythm. However, by means of this behaviour of mental neutralisation we only escape from the 'negative' consequences on our state.

There is a second possibility for the application of the law of neutralisation which I would like to propose and furthermore includes the chance to escape from polarity. We now do now fix ourselves to the bottom of the pendulum, swinging from one pole to the other, as the old Hermetics did; we now climb along the rope to the top up to the upper end where the rope of the pendulum originates. There is no movement any more because we have moved away from the level of polarity, we have transcended it. There is no distinguishing any more between male and female, plus and minus. There is total standstill, a condition which the old yogis defined as the goal of yoga:

„Yogas-chitta-vrtti-nirodhah.“
„Union is restraining the thought-streams natural to the mind .“
PYS 1,2

This guideline, this sutra as it is called in Yoga is the second guiding principle in one of the most famous teachings of yoga philosophy, the sutras of Patanjali. 'Yoga' is defined here as a condition resulting from the entire resolving (nirodha) of all movements (the translation of 'vrtti' means movement, restlessness) in the mind (chitta). Our mental movements which are thoughts, evaluations, wishes, fears etc. are forming a kind of veil (Maya), preventing us from insight into our real being. As soon as we enter the condition of entire inner peace, which according to the introduced laws must also manifest on the outside life ('As above so below. As inside so outside.'), we rest, as Patanjali writes in his next sutra, in our true being:

„Tada Drastuh Svarupe Vasthanam."
„Then the seer dwells in his own nature."
PYS 1,3

„Otherwise he is of the same form as the thought-streams."
PYS 1,4

So we learn that we normally identify with our ego-consciousness finding ourselves thrown into polarity due to mental activity/movement. We clearly see that the path to escape polarity and return to our original (divine) unity runs across the mind, across our thoughts. The closer we approach the centre, the point of neutrality, have unprejudiced, undiscriminating standpoints with regard to life the more balanced, relaxed and authentic we will be. The pendulum stops swinging and the emotional ups and downs of our feelings do not reach the usual extent.

We always have a choice: Do we want to sit on the bottom of the pendulum, experiencing the entire extent of moods from 'over the moon to down to the dumps' or do we want to reach a stable balance with even moods and consistency of emotions? Depending on what we are aiming at, what we are deeming as appropriate, we may totally identify with polar consciousness or more and more move towards neutrality.

If we want to walk the path of awaking/enlightenment, this path will lead us via the neutral mind because this condition enables us to (re-)gain consciousness of divine unity. Although at the beginning it may not be our expressive aim to reach the high peaks of enlightenment, the possibility to attain a neutral or a more and more neutral state of mind, may show us the way out of the inevitably painful polar (ego-) consciousness.

The symbol of the pendulum may be of valuable service in our daily life. If I feel emotional stress as a reaction to an exterior experience it is not important which direction I take, although we practically tend to avoid intensive drive towards the 'negative' direction I imagine the symbol of the pendulum visualising myself climbing it from the bottom to the top and remaining there, as high as I can. Safe in my new position right at the top of the pendulum I learn that the emotional wave that would have caught me otherwise is much lighter than experienced ever before. I feel that I am able to react more calmly until I at least do not have to react any more reaching the point where no outside experience drags me away from my (neutral) centre.

This, however, is not achieved overnight but considering constant practice, attentiveness and attention we will experience first improvement on this path. At this point we wish to proceed on this way, constantly supervising ourselves in our daily routine, questioning our reactions and see how the newly attained peace of mind is good for us, comfortable for our fellow-beings and leading us towards a happy and peaceful, more relaxed living.

After some time we even find out that our fears disappear because we know, there is no need to be discomposed because we have reached a level of inner balance and mental stability helping us to face life in a confident and brave way instead of trembling in fear about what life will bring us and of being thrown out of our centre by every slight deviation.

We can support this path with any form of spiritual practice, the more regular the better. Imagine a muscle we want to train. The result will be different whether training with dumb bells is done only now and then or daily. It is the same with spiritual training. I will be able to obtain fast and good results if I practise daily, even with only five to ten minutes at the beginning (eleven minutes are a perfect time span as I will explain in a subsequent book in which I shall introduce more detailed techniques).

As I proceed further on my path of spiritual development, the more I will experience inner longing for spiritual practice. Then, it will be natural for me to 'offer up' one to two hours of the day because I feel that this is the most useful I can do. It will no more be sacrifice to me; it will be the most important work of the day at which my life is aimed at more and more.

There will be a completely new quality of life; I feel that I even wish to change my life. Distracted from my most important journey, the trip to myself started with refraining from outwardly-bound pleasures and artificial entertainment like TV or media consumption, from going out and celebrating parties with friends or experiencing exotic long-distance journeys which had caught my attention before. Distracted from my most important journey, the trip to myself...

The Neutral Mind

After having deeply experienced and understood the extremes of negative and positive mind we come to a point where a balance of both can be found. As far as it is possible we avert from the world of polar opposites beginning our way back into the consciousness of unity. We no longer try to adapt the extremes, as described by the old hermetic, because thus we would still remain in the world of opposites. We create a third new state: the state of neutral mind where we do no longer have to identify with anything because we no more cling to the exterior world of appearances.

This is the way back from matter into unity: We integrate polar opposites into the eternal ONE. This is not only about balance of the two poles, it is all about integration. The neutral mind serves as the guide to the essence of our being, to the core, the divine core in us, to our soul. According to the teachings of Kundalini Yoga taught by Yogi Bhajan the neutral mind needs nine seconds to be activated serving as a basis for our decisions. This means the path leading to either positive or negative mind and reaction begins if we do no longer react automatically but first breathe deeply, waiting for nine seconds and listen inside ourselves waiting for the neutral mind to give the answer.

The neutral mind does not have to be created artificially; it is present in every human being. We all have an inner androgynous share. The principle of gender teaches us that every one of us has both the male and the female (mental) aspect and, of course, a neutral mind. To nourish and to strengthen this neutral mind, to let its qualities decide upon our lives, this is the path leading us back to divine consciousness, thus helping us to find the exit from all illusionary perception of reality. This is the attitude of mind that will no longer create Karma because it is free from any egoistic intention which is the Karma-creating factor of our actions.

Our intuition is closely connected with the neutral mind because it is coming from the heart. Our heart is working independently from polar oppositions, as we will see when it comes to our discussion of the ninth law. The intelligence of the heart is strongly connected to the neutral mind; it is our compass directly leading to our soul. The corresponding newly-attained mental clarity and relaxation helps us see our life from a superior level, the so-called Meta-level. There, we are able to see ourselves react in different situations of life leading to further sovereignty against life and helps us become solid as a rock.

The Essence of True Identity

This is the translation of 'Sat Nam Rasayan', an ancient Yogi healing technique. It must be mentioned at this point because its main instrument and essential feature is neutrality or Shunya, translated 'silence'. In neutrality our consciousness does not judge which is why at this point experience is pure and unaltered. Thus, a meditative consciousness is established in which everything can be perceived, however, without judgement and without comparing it with own memories, doubts, pictures and other mental content which may arise.

This state of consciousness can be characterized by encompassing attention and conscious attention for all feelings. In this neutral condition of consciousness we are not less sensitive, as we might assume, because we do no longer identify with our emotions. It is just the contrary: We are free to feel everything THAT IS, not allowing any emotion, which is mostly reactive and usually determined by a past trauma taking over our entire field of consciousness.

As soon as this area of neutrality and attention is restricted by the following of inner pictures or arising thoughts, we separate from current experiences replacing them by interpretations. However, the constructions thus created are part of the mental structure of the observer and are no longer neutral reality. As a consequence, the space for perception is restricted because further authentic experiences are refused leading us further away from reality into self-created worries which will totally overlap the present moment.

The Power of NOW

Neutral mind as the real meditative mind is the state of consciousness which is the goal of any spiritual practice leading us to ventures like compassion, attentiveness, presence, purity. Another way to more and more realizing the neutral mind in our lives, is practising presence in perfectness. Awareness of the present moment with our entire attention and full consciousness, resting where we are and what we are doing, what is going on around us that is what counts.

Total oneness with the present moment is directly connecting us with life, with God. It results in an entire new liveliness exceeding all of our expectations. We become ONE with life, flowing like fish in the water in the river of life, careless and carefree, knowing that every day is a present of GOD and that nothing may happen to us; that life IS.

As Patanjali wrote in its first and most important of all Sutras on Yoga:

„Atha Yoganusasanam."
„Yoga is Now."
PYS 1,1

In the NOW we see life, we see us, we see God. This NOW immediately leads us to the ninth law, to fulfilment.

9. The Law of Love

'The key stone of the pyramid is pure divine love in the form of Christos.

Any desire and all longings have been overcome; the being is resting in pure perception: Sat-Chit-Ananda (being-consciousness-blessedness). The heart unites what matter has separated; the return into the lap of God is achieved.'

WAY OF THE HEART

This principle describes the real meaning of trinity: to experience love in our universe: The acting (Father) and the inspiring spirit (Holy Spirit) create a new living spirit (Son). In this condition, the human being is an awakening conscious creative being which has been brought to the most superior form of being thus having returned to the source consciousness manifesting in our universe in the form of trinity.

The three facets/qualities of the divine in Yoga are called 'Sat-Chit-Ananda' and are a description of Brahman who normally has no characteristics. In this connection 'Sat' is the condition of being or existence in general, is highest joy and happiness, even truth. 'Chit' stands for consciousness, brain, highest knowledge/wisdom. 'Ananda' is the highest happiness, blessedness. The Upanishads say that pure joy of Brahman is the highest form of absolute happiness.

This is the condition Jesus Christ called 'God's kingdom on earth'. He meant nothing else than living in pure unconditional love, a love uniting everything, excluding nothing, unconditionally and without expectation. Then we are truthful, resting in the essence of our being, our divine core, living in 'God's kingdom'. The love that Jesus meant and taught is an unconditional divine love. It is this love we are talking about here, forming the highest of all cosmic laws which is the aim of our existence here on earth. We are living here in order to learn to love, letting it flow into all areas of our life. Thus we shall create heaven on earth as Jesus taught us.

When we rest in this one love, the three facets are not separated from each other. When we deeply dive into the inside, fixing ourselves to our (higher) heart[1], we experience these three facets altogether and know that this is the all-comprehensive love. As soon as we have realised the condition of this inner vision we really start living in the kingdom of heaven. Otherwise, the being/the existence can be found at a certain place separated from consciousness while at the same time blessedness is far away at another place which is only reached very rarely. If we experience the perception of being/consciousness/blessedness at the same moment with all qualities supplementing and completing the other, we are living in pure love. This is the place Jesus called 'kingdom of heaven/god's kingdom'.

This means that God's kingdom is really in us. We can feel and live it. This is even our aim in life here on earth. Any search, all exterior striving does not bring us any step forward; it only detracts us from our real duty.

'The kingdom of God does not come with outside activity. You will not hear saying: Look here! or Here it is! Because you see, the kingdom of God is in you.'

Lk.17:20-21

---

[1] When talking about the heart here, the energetic, subtle heart of a human being is meant, situated in the centre of the chest, on the height of the organic heart.

Love – the Non-Duality

Unless we are highly attentive, we will walk away from the divine origin leading to a swamp of fear, suffering, voracity and hatred. A condition leading to resignation, depression, despair and suicide. A condition of separation where the outside bears danger and the world is a vale of tears and the own existence seems to be useless. This is the place we are used to call hell, with his prince, the devil being the protector of duality, conflict and separation.

If we are able to live true love we are far away from polarity, we have united good and bad in our hearts and are no longer suffering from separation. We no longer exclude nothing and nobody, accept every being as of divine origin. This is the prerequisite and basic condition to enter unconditional love. As long as we still exclude something or somebody, we are living in separation and the kingdom of God remains closed to us.

This is why true love never is restricted to either only one person or a small number of persons or a thing. As long as our love is aimed at a certain person, WE DO NOT LOVE. According to its real character, true love can only be all-comprising or non-existing. Loving only a little bit or to love a limited number of persons every now and then (the own family/friends, the own people etc.) excluding all others does not have to do anything with love. This may be a variety of divine love, a small human one, a glimpse in our hearts, in which direction the goal may be found, however, it has nothing to do with love. Never ever can it be compared with true unconditional love because finally it is still based on the principle of duality.

It is of utmost importance to exactly distinguish here between true/divine love and human/dual love because only if we know the differences, if there is no more doubt regarding the unity of all being and we perceive the divine spark in all things, only then, we are able to approach true love, the goal of our earthly life.

The human kind of love in its culmination may feel similar but basically it is rooted in conditions, poverty and all kinds of fears: the fear to lose somebody or something, the fear of loneliness, the fear not to be loved or not being attractive to others. This is why human love always wants to bond other human beings, the partner, children, friends. It wants control to be sure everything is under command. Human love often is a barter trade. We give affection for loyalty and obedience. We are expecting an appropriate standard of life, provision and fulfilment of our material needs, emotional safety, constant care and attention.

The house of human love is built on sand; it will collapse during the first big downpour. Jesus told us to build our house, our life, on solid ground so that it may not be shaken. This solid ground, the rock on which we should build our house is nothing else than unconditional love. This is why this passage from the bible is, often unaware of its real meaning, being read for marriages.

Standing on the fundament of divine love nothing can shock us, no fear, no doubt will be able to come over us. We are in a state beyond suffering because we know everything is divine and deep in our hearts we feel that nothing can happen to us because we are children of god never falling deeper than his hands could hold us. No insurance in the world may give us such a high level of security; no luck whatsoever may fill us with such joy and liveliness than knowing that our house was built on a rock.

The Science of Love

Love is one of the oldest themes in the world. For love's sake wars began, the greatest myths of mankind sing about love, it provides the best income for Hollywood and countless economies are making profit of the human yearning for love. Anything we may superficially long for: richness, power and reputation; all this is just for the sake of being loved.

Science now discovers what spiritual teachers of the world have already known for centuries: Love is the most powerful force in our universe and is able to fulfil the almost impossible. It even delivers the exact measuring result that unconditional love has a frequency of 8 Hz. Among others, this has been proven by Dan Winter by means of his measuring procedure especially developed for this purpose, the Heart Link, metering the phase position between ECG and EEG. Interesting enough, this frequency, the so-called Schuhmann frequency is also corresponding to the frequency of our earth.

Meanwhile, the strong healing power of love has also been proven scientifically. The physician Larry Dossey, author of *Healing Words* and *Prayer is Good Medicine,* mentions more than 60 different studies, proving that the power of love, for example as unconditional compassionate praying has a clearly measurable healing result.

The Heart-Math institute founded by stress researcher Doc Childre was able to prove what spiritual teachers have known for centuries by means of innovative measuring techniques: 'The intelligence of the heart is the consciousness we experience if mind and body are in balance and thus in coherence.' During his studies he was able to show that if we aim our attention towards our heart and a central heart feeling like love, devotion or compassion is activated, the heart beat will immediately be more coherent resulting in a cascade of neuronal and biochemical events influencing almost all organs of the body.

Studies say that heart coherence also results in more intelligence because the activity of the sympathetic nerve system (the fight or escape reflex) is reduced and the growth stimulating parasympathetic nerve system is strengthened. Relaxation in combination with heart coherence reduces the distribution of the stress hormone Cortisol in its preliminary stages leading to the anti-aging-hormone DHEA (Dehydroepiandrosterone). Activation of heart energy by feelings of love, compassion and devotion help us live a healthier, longer and, above all, a more happy life.

Researchers of the Fels Research Institute discovered already in the 1970s that the heart has a separate, independent nerve system with at least 40.000 neurones which communicate with brain areas as the amygdale, the thalamus and the cerebral cortex which are related to consciousness. The heart does not automatically do what the brain tells it. Depending on the emotional condition of the person it interpretes the neuronal signals in its own way. This may be the aspect the French mathematician and philosopher Blaise Pascal meant as he said 'The heart has reasons which the brain does not know.'

The heart sends our emotions to our surrounding and is also influenced by the emotions others are distributing. If one person emotionally connects with others, the electrical activities of the communicating hearts start interlocking and synchronising with each other. This means that the healing vibration of the heart can be transmitted. We understand how important it is that feelings of love, compassion and happiness are sent to our surrounding. It is not only because we attract people with similar vibration because of the principle of resonance. We also encounter further experiences of joy and love thus intensifying the field of love in our world via morphological resonance helping all people to get access to these feelings.

The more we understand that the desired things we are searching for on the outside we only have to develop within ourselves, because we attract them naturally, the more we will experience the feeling of plenitude in our life. The feeling of deficit forcing us to search on the outside is replaced by the feeling of plenitude and we know that everything we are longing for is already in us. We do not need money or reputation or power to be loved, we only have to become affectionate personalities. We have to decide to proceed from 'love of power' to 'power of love'.

Characteristics Of Human Love

Human love can easily be distinguished from unconditional love. We may recognise it by having expectations and hopes, duties, the will to change others, not refraining from suppressing others. It offers achievements and expects reward which means that it is reckoning, calculating and full of intention. The results are dependencies, clinging and holding back. Its willingness to make sacrifices is wrong because the sacrifice is done for purposes of reward. There is fear to lose the other, thus producing fear.

This is a polar power because it distinguishes, separates and creates conflict and discord. Only one false word, one wrongly understood gesture may be the reason for complete switching, love changing into bitter hatred. This is why human beings say: 'Love and hatred are very close to each other.' Like any polar thing has its opposite human love also has its opposite.

Before we know it, jealousy, disappointment, frustration and separation come up. Love is always closely related to loss, loneliness and bitterness often ending in aggression, violence, sickness and death.

Following the law of polarity and the law of rhythm, human love never leads to constant happiness, it only brings passing feelings of happiness, highs followed by lows. Like ebb and flood, day and night follow each other the ecstasy of love ends in the depth of disappointment and frustration. This happens if I do not obtain what I expected from my beloved partner or if it does not happen as I imagined it. This love is like a bird, jumping from one branch to another, wandering from one to another...

Characteristics of Unconditional Love

To LOVE unconditionally means to have Jesus Christ resurrected in our heart. When Jesus said, 'I am the path, the truth and the life', he demanded to follow him and to live in unconditional love, in constant prayer, as he did. It is not only real saints like him and distant Yogis who are able to do this. We all have the ability. We all are children of God thus having the ability to unconditionally love in us.

We approach this ability if we live the values and orders all great religions and spiritual traditions tell us instead of only preaching them. The most important point here is non-violence, as it is called in Yoga, the uppermost order, 'Ahimsa'. It comprises respect for life, not only for the life of other people but as well for the life of animals and respect for creation in general. We are living a modest life not using more than we need and thus, neither living at the expense of others nor exploiting others. Our modesty is the result of the experience of plenitude, knowing that I will always have enough to earn a living. It is a perception beyond deficiency that would greedily push me to strive for more and more because of the fear of not having enough. And there is modesty humbly receiving the gifts God is presenting, sharing them brotherly and sisterly and in generosity with our fellow beings, driven by compassion and helpfulness, freely giving, giving oneself, without expectation and selfishness.

This is followed by the order of sincerity, meaning to live fully in line with the laws of the universe: An honesty meaning much more than not to lie, which is totally based upon the truthfulness of the own being thus resulting in unbreakable consistency and reliability. This love does not sway with the wind; it is solidly following the WAY OF THE HEART, the path of truth. This reliability comes from discipline which knows how to master the own desires and wishes not placing them before the rights of others. It is based on a feeling for justice and righteousness which are a natural result of mercy on the path of love.

A further feature of unconditional love is the freedom from all inside and outside pressures, freedom from all deficiency and perfect peace in all-comprising tranquillity of the heart. This love leads to balance and the unswerving feeling of being at your centre point, relaxedness, peace in all doings not knowing any stress and hectic.

The reason for all this is persistence and steadiness in doing what has to be done, what can be done at a given time; however, all this without expectation which is the reason why I do not have to fear disappointment. This is a perseverance following the laws of life with utmost flexibility and inner agility without reacting on any outward expectations. It is like water flowing around a stone, like a living branch bending without breaking in the storms of life.

Further characteristics of unconditional love:

- Purity, not only of the body but mainly purity of our thoughts, feelings and actions which only then are pure if they are in accordance with the divine order, based on the order of charity, also comprising love for oneself.
- Satisfaction leading to inner rest, gentleness and steadiness as firmness of the heart because it is free from any desire.
- Spontaneity, openness and trust in God, absolutely aware of being totally safe and in utmost well-being.

Unconditional love does not classify and evaluate, it does not judge or condemn and it is free of judgement, merciful and forgiving. It leads us to freedom, peace, happiness, harmony, growth, dignity and perfection.

The character and the essence of all being is revealed to us and merges with the sense of our being. As Antoine de Saint-Exupéry wrote in 'The Little Prince':

'One can only see clearly with the heart, the essence is hidden from the eyes.'

The Vivid Aspect of Unconditional Love

Joy is an essential vivid expression of love and may be a most valuable guide to unconditional love. As soon as we do something with joy we are doing it unconditionally and the feeling of vividness grows. If there is joy behind all our actions instead of ego-driven desire we are on our way to make heaven on earth a reality. When our acting is driven by the thought of joy and we are completely consecrated to this service without any outside aim like increasing our turnover or to qualify for a managing position, our acting will be radiant with vividness exceeding any busy working by far.

Blessedness will grow in us which the American scientist and happiness researcher Mihalyi Csikszentmihalyi also called 'Flow' and which has always been able to create the real big achievements of mankind. Csikszentmihalyi found out: 'I have observed artists, composers, athletes and scientists who absolutely love their profession never wanting to do anything else but what they are doing.

They do not do it because they are expecting rewards. They do not do it for money or even reputation. Even recognition by colleagues is not important to them. They do it because it is important for themselves bringing them lots of happiness and fulfilment; nothing in the world may be compared to this experience. The most amazing to me is that this kind of absolute dedication to something which makes life liveable can be chosen from a vast variety of different topics.'

Even normally unpleasant everyday-tasks like cleaning the toilet, sorting accounting documents or ironing shirts can be carried out with a feeling of dedication and service thus increasing their appreciation and changing our point of view regarding such tasks. A simple change in our attitude makes the difference: Instead of expecting joy from the things we are doing or to think that joy would be a result of our activities, it is more vice versa: The joy in us will flow into what we are doing. This way any activity will become a joyful experience.

The most important thing is to be totally involved making the present moment the centre of our lives. The degree to which we achieve this, our ability to experience joy will increase and we will stop running after joyful amusements.

It is not the goal we wish to achieve with our activity but the activity itself revealing the deep emotion of liveliness. If we are performing something we experience the dynamic aspect of love which connects us with the energy all existence is based upon.

Joy helps us to be one with the universal creative power thus serving life. Serving must not be understood in the usual sense of 'being served by a waiter' where we are literally denying our own task in life in order to subdue to the ego-purposes of another human being in a kind of compulsory labour. In this context, serving means fulfilment of the own task of life, the own sense of life. The extent to which we can free ourselves from all exterior goals presented by our brain and social influences totally merging with the meaning of our lives, to this extent we will be servants of creation finding the kind of fulfilment on earth our soul is longing for.

As long as we get distracted from the temptations of the ego, nourished from exterior goals either because of own needs or the needs of our surrounding, we will never find our true aim in life and will not experience the luck we are expecting from the fulfilment of our desires. We may collect all the money and the power of the world without being happy afterwards. We may delude our brain or other people; however, we cannot cheat our soul. She always knows whether we are following the path of the soul or whether we are following exterior delusions and temptations.

We will experience deep confidence and never ending joy even with totally unspectacular activities if we are dedicated to our task of life making it the most important aim of our life. Unless we are ready to leave everything behind us which has promised safety and happiness, only then we are ready to serve supreme tasks. This is meant by the sayings of enlightened beings telling us that we must be prepared to die before we can really start living. Here, they do not talk about the physical death, but about the death of the ego obstructing the way to our real self as long as we have not freed ourselves from its chains.

Imagine we would live in a world where all human beings have freed themselves from the chains of the ego, living in perfect harmony with their higher self, acknowledging the true sense of their lives? What would such a world look like? Would there be greed for power, money and reputation which lead our planet to the abyss we are standing now, neither moving backward or forward. Would people unscrupulously murder others, enslave and cheat them? Would we devastate our environment, torture and abuse our animal brothers and sisters? Would you think a human being, a man who is in harmony with his soul might act this way?

All problems we encounter on the exterior have their origin in the fact that we have left the creative flow of being. We have bound ourselves with the wrong goals of the ego, denying the real sense of our lives. If we are seriously longing for a better, equal world we must at first start with ourselves, revealing the true sense of our lives, taking the courage to live according to this. Only then, we will invite all the situations and humans into our lives which help us to realise the goal of our life, because we are in resonance with them, attracting them naturally because we feel their vibration among thousands of differently swinging human beings.

If we decide to realise the true goal of life and practice complete dedication we will reach the corresponding high heart coherence and pure vibration of the heart energy. When we have reached this condition, acting in harmony with our higher self, our actions will be incomparably brighter and stronger than every busy acting resulting from the desire of the ego. Then we are acting because of pure happiness of doing, then we lead a real godly life, as expresses the famous 9th symphony of Beethoven:

'Joy, oh what a godly sparking, daughter of Elysium,
drunk with fire we're embarking, blissful, in your holy room.

Your spell's magic mends each other's ties our customs strictly breach,
all the people will be brothers where your gentle wing shall reach.'

The Philosopher's Stone

Unconditional love is more than a feeling, it is a state of being. It is an attitude of life that comprises everything, not only joy, but also the so-called 'enemy', the animals, the plants, mother earth, even darkness, the abysses and fear. It leads us to a condition where we feel connected with all and as part of creation we perceive God as a living truth in our hearts. It is the breath of life, the living/holy spirit that lets our hearts glow, filling all our words and deeds with the deep power of creativity.

Unconditional love can never be disappointed because it does not expect anything. It does not know pain, suffering, it is beyond sorrow, fear and depression. Not judging, it expects and demands nothing. The closest of all forms of human love is a mother's love which is very close to unconditional love because a mother loves her children no matter what they do and how they are. She loves unconditionally making them the biggest gift we may experience in this world. He who has once experienced unconditional love knows that there is nothing bigger, more beautiful, more perfect and more desirable. He will always remember and yearn at the bottom of his heart for these times. This experience is the basic reason of the human striving for unconditional love in its highest form, the divine love, where it is all-comprising.

In silent hours we remember this experience wishing deep in our hearts to be able again to rest at mother's breast feeling her unconditional love. We often forget that we are called to realize this love thus becoming godlike. He who gives will be given. Who LOVES will be LOVED. The law of vibration will always be applied in order to fulfil the most superior aim of our being, the fulfilment of our deepest longing. The longing for the return to our divine origin.

Unconditional love is a power that cannot be misused because it does not know enemy, fear or doubt. It does not want to create conflict, not taking advantage at the cost of others. It gives without expectation although it is the most supreme power in the world. It is able to move mountains, make impossible things possible and do so-called miracles. Just as Jesus untiringly encouraged us: 'You will do all I have done, yes, even bigger things than these.' This is why love is the most supreme power helping us to be in harmony with the creative powers of the universe.

Our is therefore the will of God and will undoubtedly be fulfilled. This is the magic of love, the biggest secret among all secrets and therefore the real key stone of the pyramid. The philosopher's stone for which all adepts and searchers of this world have ever looked for.

The Magic of the Heart

Unconditional love is the most supreme healing power because it is sacred power coming from the heart. This means that it is beyond separation which is the reason for any suffering and every disease. Disease arises if we separate each other from our divine core/from our soul thus forming blockages in our subtle fine energy system. This means that the energy of life, the basis for the proper functioning of all organs in the human body cannot flow unhindered. When we are in the unconditional love, energy blockings and thus all our complaints and diseases will dissolve. Any suffering vanishes bit by bit and we are radiant of energy and joy of life.

Unconditional love is able to lift the frequency of our vibrations to the highest possible level which means that we only attract what is in harmony with this high-vibration frequency. Any bad luck, disease and suffering will not encounter us any more because these conditions are on a much lower frequency. Unconditional love is able to overcome any low vibration. In its presence, even darkness is without chance: Like in a dark room in which the light is switched on, unconditional love takes over.

It is the highest power in universe and there is nothing beyond. It can change everything, heal everything and create everything. Unconditional love is also the secret of everlasting health and eternal youth. Unconditional love is real magic: changing our entire experience, our self, our life and the world as a whole. It eradicates all disharmonies in our life so that we will encounter only loving people and are free from problems. We are totally protected as soon as we **are** unconditional love. Nothing will be harmful for us: no attack, no accident, no theft and no catastrophe whatsoever. All our wishes will come true. We will be given the gifts of life becoming one with the sense of our life. As the great wisdom teacher Patanjali writes in his famous Yoga-Sutras:

"In the presence of one firmly established in non-violence, all hostilities cease."
PYS 2.35

"To one established in truthfulness, actions and their results become sub-servient."
PYS 2.36

"To one established in non-stealing, all wealth comes."
PYS 2.37

"When non-greed is confirmed, a thorough illumination of the how and why of one's birth comes."
PYS 2.39

This is what unconditional love is about: We are in the most supreme state of being. We do no longer need laws, no ten commandments, not even the spiritual laws. Because love is the highest of laws thus bearing all the others in itself standing above all laws and becoming a law itself. We might even say: 'All is allowed, love the law.' or, with the words of Jesus 'Thou shall love thy master, your God with all of your heart, all of your soul and all of your thoughts. That is the most important and first order.' In the condition of unconditional love we are one with God, synchronically swinging on the highest frequency in universe. We are all light, because where love is there is light and vice versa. We are in heaven walking in the light of God:

"I do not pray for these only, but also for those who believe in me through their word, that they may all be one; even as you, Father, are in

me, and I in you, that they also may be in us, so that the world may be-
lieve that you have sent me. The glory which you have given me I have
given to them, that they may be one even as we are one, I in them and
you in me, that they may become perfectly one, so that the world may
know that you have sent me and have loved them even as you have loved
me.
Father, I desire that they also, whom you have given me, may be with me
where I am, to behold my glory which you have given me in your love for
me before the foundation of the world. O righteous Father, the world has
not known you, but I have known you; and these know that you have sent
me. I made known to them your name, and I will make it known, that the
love with which you have loved me may be in them, and I in them."
Johannes 17, 20 – 26

The Path to Unconditional Love

It is the sense of our life on earth to attain the condition of unconditional love thus freeing ourselves from the wheel of Karma, the
circle of birth and rebirth, returning to the divine unity. Love is the
aim of all of us, our sense of being and our fulfilment. The path
through the incarnations always confronts us with situations helping us to understand this and to see the light through all the experiences of separation and suffering. Only he who has experienced
darkness knows what light is. Only who has experienced the night
can see the day, only who has gone through fear will understand
love.

Now we have learned that our so-called opponents, enemies and
people making life hard for us are our best teachers. It is exactly their
intention to open our eyes for light and love through the experiencing of suffering, grief and separation. Instead of encountering these
people with disagree, hatred or aggression we should be thankful,
caring and looking at what we shall experience and learn with them.

But what do we do mostly in such situations? We act according to our usual patterns, pitying ourselves that these people are able to torture us developing all kinds of defense against them, from disappointed heart to aggressive violence. This is what we are doing all our life until, finally in old age, we are turning our back to the world filled with bitterness and hatred.

Those 'difficult' situations of life are the most important mile stones to get insight in ourselves by being taught unconditional love, quickly growing and transforming. This is possible by means of a conscious mental process using our will in situations where normally an automatic defensive reaction starts, looking inward and then no longer follow our usual patterns but react totally different meaning that we do **not** react for several breaths long. We then take deep breaths several times waiting for the outcome of the situation, let negative thoughts pass by without reacting to them, waiting for the things to come.

At this point our positive mind takes over revealing to us the possibilities of growth with this situation, showing us which potential of inner transformation may be included. After reasonable time (the nine seconds mentioned) our neutral mind will come up with a suitable reaction.

We now decide to further love the person who hurt, offended, cheated and thus disappointed us deeply, because this is the aspect we want to learn. The so-called terrible and painful situation will change into magical transformation for us. This is exactly the magic of the heart overcoming any pain, separation and grief, healing it and lifting us to a supreme level of spiritual maturity. This is why Jesus said: 'Love your enemies!'

However, this requires high attentiveness and mindfulness as well as a large amount of humility and devotion. These all are values characterised by unconditional love. These values were of course not put into our cradle. We are at a point of human evolution where this mostly must be learned in detail until they have become a fixed part of our life so that we are able to access them in the most crucial and demanding situations of life.

This is why regular spiritual practices like praying, meditation and yoga are indispensable points on the path towards unconditional love, to the awakening from illusionary painful perception of reality. In my subsequent book I will show practical knowledge based on the spiritual laws and the WAY OF THE HEART with detailed and precise techniques taken from Kundalini Yoga. The realisation of this practice will show verifiable and predictable success.

Love abounds in all things,
excels from the depths to beyond the stars,
is lovingly disposed to all things.
She has given the king on high
the kiss of peace.

Hildegard of Bingen

A PATH OF AWAKENING

Mind, Matter and Love

The WAY OF THE HEART is a path of awakening which is defined as the path of the middle, the path of truth. The golden mean was already defined as truth by the ancient wise men from the Far East, especially since Confucius, who revealed it as being the truth. In his sustainably impressing philosophy Confucius tried to see opposites in their conditionality thus uniting them from a supreme point of view. Even long before, Hermes Trismegistus determined in his spiritual laws, especially in the law of polarity the centre as being the point where we are able to recognize truth. Thus, we read in the Kybalion:

"... like and unlike are the same; opposites are identical in nature, but different in degree; extremes meet; all truths are but half-truths; all paradoxes may be reconciled."

Walking the WAY OF THE HEART we are taking up the thread and make an important step forward. We are showing that the path of the middle which has already been recognized as the path of truth, is also a WAY OF THE HEART. This step is meaningful because with its help and by means of our (subtly fine) heart and its qualities and abilities we can find a way to truth, a path to God because god is truth. This means that the WAY OF THE HEART is a path to awakening, which via the centre, our heart, is leading to the truth.

The WAY OF THE HEART is built on the spiritual laws and amends them by the law of neutralisation and the law of love. It changes the sequence of the preceding laws in one position, namely by putting the law of cause and action from place 6 to place 3.

With this sequence the principles form the circle of creation: from the mind down to matter and via the all-comprising divine love back into the all-comprising divine mind. The laws 1 to 3 deal with the mental basics of our universe, the basic principles according to which all being is organised. They are therefore also called the laws of the mind describing how duality and matter were created from (divine) unity.

The laws 4 to 6 explain according to which rules matter is organised and functions. They are serving as explanation of all procedures in matter, also including invisible forms like thoughts, feelings, physical forces and energies. They are thus called the laws of matter.

Finally, the laws 7 to 9 explain how we achieve the escape from duality, polarity, the level of matter back to divine unity. They are therefore commonly called the laws of love.

1. The law of mentalism
2. The law of correspodance
3. The law of cause and action
4. The law of vibration
5. The law of polarity
6. The law of of rhythm
7. The law of of gender
8. The law of neutralisation
9. The law of love

The Circle of Creation

There is a beautiful metaphor from yoga philosophy which gives us an impression of the circle of creation, the path the divine took in matter and where the wish to return into the divine unity comes from. It is exactly this striving for reunion, which is called 'religio' in its original sense or 'yoga', which is the reason for the spiritual search of man which can be traced back to the earliest beginnings of humankind, back to the caves of the Stone Age.

'It says that before creation there was nothing but the pure shapeless and unmanifest being in which Shiva, standing for consciousness, and Shakti, the divine energy, are one. In this condition the wish came up to experience oneself in the world of shape. While Shiva with his transcendent, resting aspect remained unchanged as pure consciousness, Shakti starts separating from him as a dynamical and creative power. This is the first step into duality. Shakti is pulsed by Nada (sound; symbolised by 'OM') and from this the mind, the language and all things are created. However, in the following period Shakti wraps herself more and more in Maya (the 'world of phenomena'), thus experiencing that she is more and more separated from Shiva.

After Shakti has created mind and body of the human being and all things, her creative process is finished, she rolls up and rests. Nevertheless, her consciousness of unity with Shiva and thus the longing to get back to the condition of unity remain. This longing expresses itself as spiritual search in human beings. For most human beings, however, the veils of Maya are so tight, so veiling that this longing is expressed in a search for satisfaction of the senses, luxury, richness and so on while getting deeper and deeper involved in the net of Maya, the world of phenomena.

Regarding the human astral body this corresponds to the process of creation; and the separation between Shakti and Shiva means the decline of the

human energetic and spiritual potential from the highest chakra at the po-
sition of the apex point on the head (Sahasrara) which is associated with
consciousness of Shiva through all chakras down to the Muladhara Chakra
on the pelvic floor. Every chakra which Shakti is descending within human
consciousness means deeper involvement in rough categories of being. If all
human levels of experience have unveiled which means a total alienation
from divine origin and nature, Shakti rests in the bottom chakra as potential
divineness, as latent spiritual energy.

This spiritual or awakening energy is called 'kundalini'. The different
techniques of hatha and Kundalini Yoga make it possible to wake up the
power of kundalini from its 'Sleeping-Beauty' slumber guiding them
through the different chakras upward, back to their real truth, divine or
Shiva-consciousness.

In her ascent Shakti withdraws all her strength from Maya (exterior
world, world of illusion): With every further step the veil of ignorance is
taken away bit by bit; man recognises his true being even more precise. The
world in its former shape is dissolving; with every step on the way man is
raising his state of consciousness, becoming more and more one with the
world of divineness. This state of 'coming home' is called Samadhi, the cos-
mic consciousness.[2]

This metaphor of separation of Shakti and Shiva shows the circle
of creation as an image which is finally nothing more than a circle of
vibrations. As Shakti moves through the chakras, the subtle fine-en-
ergy centres of human beings, from the bottom where she had as-
cended up to the highest of steps, the connection with the divine aspect, thus reuniting with Shiva, the same way we can ascend by lifting our level of frequency from the deepest point of total identifica-

---

[2] From „Vision of Yoga" by Arjuna P. Nahtschläger

tion of our consciousness with matter to the connection with the supreme consciousness (unconditional love) uniting with our divine self. This way, we may awake from the illusionary dream and become able to walk the path of enlightenment.

The re-unification between Shakti and Shiva, the unification of the individual soul with the divine soul began with the 7th law, the principle of gender. The separation which started in the 2nd law, the principle of correspondance, is now neutralized. The (spiral) circle is closing in order to gush again into the form. This spiral circle is the explanation why evolution bears a direction: an evolution and sublime development, forward and upward. The spiral shape ascension makes development possible, it is even inevitably connected with the form. Every circle of creation bears the benefit of experience and thus further development. Although after every circle we return to the original condition, we are not the same we used to be at the beginning of our journey. We return, however, we are changed, richer in experience, thus ascending one step of the ladder of evolution.

The form of the spiral is closely connected with evolution which is why we can find it everywhere in nature as for example from snails, sun flowers, spider webs, the DNS of our genes to the planets, galaxies and spiral nebula. The spiral is a symbol of the universe and of creation and can also be found as holy symbol in several old cultures. Ritual dances were often performed in spiral form where the in and out often was a symbol of death and 'resurrection', i.e. re-incarnation. However, it was also a symbol of transience of all earthly matter and a symbol of the path of the human being coming from the light (God) into darkness (solid matter) and ascending from darkness (solid matter) back into light by overcoming his/her the individual Karma. The clockwise turning spiral is the symbol of evolution, the development of matter, because it flows from the inside to the outside while the left-hand spiral is a sign of involution, the return to unity, flowing from the outside back to the inside.

WAY OF THE HEART- A Path of Truth

The path of the middle is the path to God because it is a path of truth as the centre is the truth. It is the point where the two opposite poles of reality meet, the point in which we are at a neutral point, not tending to either of the sides but uniting and balancing the two extremes. It is neither black nor white, neither darkness nor light. It is both and nothing of both. It is the point of compensation, of calmness and silence. There is no more movement here because movement needs energy and in the zero point the energy is equal to zero. The extremes neutralize each other as from duality we return to unity thus returning to god.

The path of the middle is also the WAY OF THE HEART because it is the character of the heart, to unite, to achieve reconciliation of polar opposites, to bring about peace, to sow love. The heart wants to overcome dispute and achieve unity. All contradictions are resolving in the heart because the heart loves unconditionally. It is the brain that sets conditions and expectations which the heart does of course not know because it only knows love. We believe being able to control everything with the assistance of our brain. However, it is a fact that our consciousness is only able to capture a tiny fraction of all information (stimuli) available in our organism. The organism does the most of it, however, the consciousness does not take any notice. The heart, however, reacts upon many unconscious stimuli.

Our brain is nothing more than a storage device. All that is stored is old; never is it new; never is it original. It is a biological computer determined for certain purposes as for collecting, classification, storage and later demand of knowledge. The intelligence of the heart brings poetry to our life, inspires our actions and fills our life with festivity and joy. It gives us the laughing and the ability to love or to share anything with others. Life can only unfold by means of our heart which is the nourishing soil on which all beauty and all truly valuable aspects are growing. It is the centre of our being, our middle, our truth.

Truth is the language of the heart because our heart is able to distinguish truth from lie. Our brain would be overburdened, because it can only decide upon rational aspects and because it is not able to perceive subtle fine vibrations. Our heart is able to distinguish vibrations and feel emotions entering into resonance with other vibrations, thus perceiving truth and unmask lies. This is the ability of the (subtle fine) heart in the centre of our body, in the centre of the chest beneath the   sternum. It is the centre between our subtle fine energy centres between earth and 'heaven' and unites them. It is our gate to god where we wish to centre our being, where we will find rest, peace and truth.

A Path of Awakening

A path of awakening is a predetermined path which can be used for further spiritual development in order to proceed from the dual consciousness (material) to the consciousness of unity, the highest and pure mind and truth of God. There are many ways to God; however, all of them end up in the heart leading through love.

The path introduced here as the *WAY OF THE HEART* is one of them. It is based on the spiritual laws of the Kybalion which form the basis for all religions of the world and big spiritual traditions. There is nothing essential in them which may not be traced back to the spiritual laws or, in their enlarged version, to the *WAY OF THE HEART.*

The WAY OF THE HEART thus is an instrument of reconciliation of all religions, reuniting of science and spirituality, insight and distinguishing of truth and illusion. Under its guidance, we will understand how divine consciousness found its way from the condition of unity, the pure mind, into solid matter, and we learn about the laws matter follows until we finally return from matter, the condition of duality, back into unity, the divine condition, the condition of pure mind. This mind is an all-comprising tool for learning, the development of differentiation leading us to the awakening.

The laws of the mind describe how divine consciousness in its first condition is pure mind (principle of mentalism) which, because he wanted to start the process of creation, began to 'think about himself' thus creating a model of himself (principle of correspondence). Finally, he added temporality in order to create movement and benefits from experience (the principle of cause and action). This way, the laws of mind lead us from pure mind, the condition of unity into matter, i.e. polarity.

We learn that the laws of mind form the initial understanding and the basis according to which our universe is organised. The law of correspondence and the law of cause and action give us the fundamental instruments helping us to understand what we would otherwise not be able to understand. With their help we may have the chance 'to have a glimpse at God's cards', see through the paths of fate and get insight in ourselves.

While the laws of the mind deal with the mental basics of our universe, the laws of matter describe rules according to which all matter functions, also comprising thoughts, feelings and all forms of energy and power, thus gaining championship over matter. The law of vibration explains to us how our attitude decides upon the quality of our thoughts and feelings and how we are able to draw into our life anything we desire just by having a corresponding level of frequency. The same applies to all we do not want to have in our life that is not useful for us. Now we also understand in which way we attract-certain events and experiences into our lives.

The law of polarity helps us to understand that everything in life has two sides. We get insight into the integral view of reality. The law of rhythm helps us gaining insight in the natural ups and downs of life, to transcend them to a certain amount by mastering their influence on our consciousness. The laws of matter thus help us deeply understand the material level and master it which is part of our aim in life here on earth. We have to land first before we are able to ascend; we have to land in matter before we can transcend it. The denial of matter leads to a decline as it does not help us to approach God, because matter also is divine and if we deny this, we deny God's work.

In the end, we get back into the divine lap by means of the laws of love. The starting point is the law of gender explaining the basic condition for the development of creative power thus giving us the key for the development of our own creative power. With the idea of (sexual) unification of the female and the male pole it already paves the way back from polarity to unity.

The law of neutrality consequently continues this path by neutralising both poles thus cancelling them. Moreover, it delivers a valuable means to strengthen the neutral aspect of our mind so that it is at our disposal as a servant in the overcoming of the dual view.

This means we now have a tool to transform our consciousness for spiritual insight - in every situation of our daily life.

Last but not least the sublime law, the law of love is the last link to perform the last big step back into divine consciousness, back into unity, into the light from which we came from. This law transcending all others and becoming a law itself is the top secret among all secrets which will now become our living reality so that we will be able to fulfil the incredible experiment of creation to a glorious ending. Sat Nam.

Practice

Why Spiritual Practice?

If we wish to enlarge our consciousness in order to fulfil our evolutionary order a regular spiritual practice is essential. Just as we have to train our muscles to gain more physical power we have to train our mind if we want to develop consciousness. Reading books on these topics is important and good. However, there is no use to all that knowledge on spiritual development if we do not practice. There will be no further development if I do not practise just as my muscles do not grow while I only read books on muscle training on my sofa.

Basically, our mind is nothing more than a computer. It runs the programmes it has been equipped with. Our programmes are life experience and reaction patterns we have developed in our experiences. Childhood traumas experienced over many incarnations are ending up in strategies and automatic reaction patterns to avoid bad future experiences. If there is a similar stimulus from our environment our mental computer remembers the sustained injury and reacts automatically without being conscious in a way to protect us from further painful experience.

These automatic patterns of reaction and strategies of avoidance are deeply embedded in our unconsciousness and responsible for the fact that we always act 'blindly' and in the same way, if critical situations arise. We are unable to perceive the situation as it is and remember how a similar situation used to be, thus acting accordingly. Of course we then react with an old reaction pattern which is totally inappropriate in the current situation. As a consequence the same experiences are repeated on, because we use the old pattern again and again which we have only developed because we fear injury or pain. We remain stuck in our consciousness and in our behaviour having no chance for further development.

To be willing to escape the circle of unnecessary reactive patterns and bad habits is a very practical reason for doing spiritual exercise. In order to practise this I do not necessarily have to have the longing for enlightenment or the merging with the divine consciousness in me.

Important Aspects of Spiritual Practice

Just like a muscle gets stronger the more I train it, my progress on the path to transforming or awakening consciousness will be the faster the more often I practise the necessary exercises. Regarding this aspect the mind follows the same laws as solid matter.

But not only frequency but also the duration of the exercises are important. It is a big difference whether I only train three minutes or three hours a day. This of course makes sense to us and it is no difference whether a muscle is trained or any other ability like playing the piano, driving a car, learning a foreign language shall be learned or the mind shall be trained. The longer we exercise the faster we will achieve our aim.

One further element is regularity of the exercise. It is more useful to practise half an hour daily instead of three hours once a week. Daily repetition applied to both, the muscle cell and the brain cell, means to condition the brain cells thus attaining a higher training effect. Moreover, regular repetition within a circadian rhythm (24-hours-rhythm) has even more effects and will give shape to our body clock thus literally helping us tick newly.

Additionally to frequency, duration and regularity two further essential factors must be obeyed in our spiritual practice: concentration and dedication. From the time of our school and study life we know that those were the easiest subjects to learn we enjoyed learning, which we gave our full attention, concentration and enthusiasm. Just like learning foreign languages, mathematics, chemical rules etc. concentration and dedication are decisive aspects in spiritual practise as they decide upon how big our spiritual harvest is which results from our efforts. Energy follows attention: The more attentive and concentrated I am the more energy I get from my system supporting successful progress.

"Practice becomes firmly grounded when it has been cultivated for a long time, uninterruptedly, with earnest devotion."
PYS 1,14

All aspects mentioned demand for one thing: discipline. Discipline is the basic demand for all those who want to see clear progress on the path of spiritual development. Some of us do certainly not want to hear this thinking; it is not up-to-date, however, nothing could be truer. Without discipline there is no success. Discipline is the effort, the consistency, the thoughtfulness in order to proceed on my path of spiritual development. Discipline helps us to overcome all hindrances on our path to build up spiritual practice in order to 'firmly establish' our practise as Patanjali describes it.

Though discipline alone will not help us reach our aim. Like anything in a polar world, discipline requires its opposite to be whole. This is why on our spiritual path we need the ability to let go in the right moments which means to overcome our clinging to a certain theme. These two aspects, discipline and letting go and not being attached, are in close relation to each other and we have to find out about how to develop and use them properly in order to build our progress on the path of spiritual development powerful and sustainably.

Letting go or not being attached gives us the ability to refrain from thoughts, feelings, actions and conditions of consciousness of which we know that they are not useful for us, but on the contrary: They hamper our development. We all know the famous 'belief-behaviour-gap', the gap keeping us from realising things we have experienced as being important. This gap seems to be almost insurmountable as long as we stick to our harmful habits unable to let them go. Be it customs of thinking, feeling or acting or be it our attitudes: The same mechanism applies to all of them. As long as we are not able to refrain from them they have control of our lives, with all the inconvenient consequences on our life and on our spiritual progress.

Thus, the ability being able to desist from harmful habits is the indispensable counterpart of discipline in order to achieve our aim of further spiritual progress and transformation of our consciousness. We are in need of both, just as man and woman need each other and vice versa, in order to create new life. We need discipline and let go, to create in us a new consciousness. Patanjali writes in his Sutras:

"These mental modifications are restrained by practice and non-attachment."
PYS 1.12

„Practice is the effort to maintain the cessation of thought."
PYS 1.13

„Non-attachment is self-mastery; it is freedom from desire for what is seen or heard.“
PYS 1.15

These two poles do not only require each other they even coincide mutually. If I am able to develop discipline I will be able to overcome my adherence and to free myself from behaviour which I have recognised as being useless for me, my life and my surrounding. The developed discipline will help me to overcome the insurmountable gap between the desired condition and my present state of being. Non-adherence may support the development of discipline as it helps us to defeat the lack of willpower.

If we use these two aspects in the right way, constantly and consciously, there will be nothing which we would not be able to achieve. They are the basis on which we can build our creative power, the fertile soil on which the germ we are sowing with our spiritual practice then grows to be a beautiful plant, not only changing our life from scratch but also become a benefit for our environment and the world.

Stages of Spiritual Development

In the beginning we must force ourselves to practise the exercises we have chosen again and again. Therefore, it is necessary to develop willpower in order to overcome outer and inner resistors trying to keep us away from our practice. This striving is the step we have to take and which will result in the fact that God will approach us in ten steps. Divine mercy is like fuel which is always available; personal striving is the ignition of the fuel.

After this first phase we come to a step where striving is no longer the focal point. We are literally longing for our practice to be carried out. At the point where our will has lead to the installation of a habit the sweat we shed becomes sweet nectar changing our life in a magical way from the inside.

Awaking in the morning we even do not ask ourselves whether it would not be nicer to stay in bed and still sleep a while. It is just the same as if we ask ourselves whether it were useful to no longer brush our teeth in the morning. We even were not able to start a day without our spiritual practise. It is then a firm part of our life, even part of us.

Our sub-consciousness is newly conditioned. Instead of placing stones on the path of our spiritual development we are furthermore driven to fulfil promises we gave our soul. What was daily fight between the call of the soul and convenience of our lower self has now become an integral part of our life which is as unmissable and central as breathing in and out, even like life itself. We are re-birthing ourselves, a 'new' ego in us, an ego that has always been there because it is our true ego our (higher) self which was only hidden by the veils of our (lower) ego, the non-acknowledging of our true ego.

This new life wants to unfold in its full size and beauty. Like a butterfly resting in the caterpillar escapes his narrow cocoon simply by leaving it behind like an old dress that is no longer in harmony with the new feeling of life. And at a given time, our true ego will reveal and overcome all our karmic entanglements, bringing the divine being sleeping in us into existence.

Place, Time and Duration

We are living in the dimension of space and time. This aspect must be clearly obeyed in our spiritual practice. It is decisive for us to choose properly and this should never be underestimated.

The room or the place on one hand is the outer space which we have to form in a way that it supports our exercise best. Every object being in there should be carefully chosen and not only be there by coincidence but because of a clear decision that it is useful. Colour and form are as important as the origin of the objects and what is connected with them as well as the state of consciousness they reflect. All those are energies, subtle fine vibrations which naturally have their reaction. Not to obey them would be foolish as their impact is large.

Even more important than the outside space is the inner space. How does my inner space look like when I start spiritual practice? Did I clean and tidy out properly? What about my thoughts and feelings? Do I practise with joy and dedication or with doubt or even reluctance? Am I concentrated and totally connected with what I am thinking and doing or am I somewhere else? My inner space is always with me. It helps me independently from the surrounding even in advert places, on journeys in small hotel rooms, squeezed between furniture, in the dining room with friends; even in airports I can freely practise my exercises. We are surrounded by our microcosm, no matter how our surrounding looks like.

The best time for spiritual practice is 2.5 hours before sunrise because the angle in which the sun is standing related to the earth at that time is especially supportive for spiritual activity. During this time, there is more Prana (vital energy), the world is still sleeping the noise of the day has not yet started. To leave the bed at that time means benefiting from high quality of practice because our body now supports physical cleaning even better than during the day or in the evening. For most of the people this is the biggest problem. However, when we have become used to this habit, it will be normal soon because the fruit we earn are more than worthwhile.

We may also prepare our body by taking a cold shower immediately upon getting up. This has not only the effect that we are full of energy, it also supports the cleaning processes by eliminating poisonous substances from our blood and by concentrated breathing they can also be removed by our lungs.

The period of time we spend with our spiritual exercise is firstly depending on the circumstances of life but mainly on our aims and on our seriousness. Anything from three minutes until several hours a day is possible here. The science of yoga has found that the following exercise periods are needed for certain desired effects in meditation:

- 3 minutes of meditation affects the electromagnetic field, influences the circulation and stability of the blood
- 11 minutes of meditation begins to change the glandular and nervous system
- 22 minutes of meditation balances and coordination the three functional minds – the positive, negative and neutral mind – and they begin to work together
- 31 minutes of meditation allows the glands, breath, and concentration to affect all cells and rhythms of the body and all layers of the mind`s projection.

- 62 minutes of meditation changes the gray matter of the brain; integrates the subconscious "shadow mind" and the external projection of the mind.
- 2 1/2 hours of meditation changes the psyche in it's co-relation with the surrounding magnetic field, so that the subconscious mind is firmly held in the new ways of thinking and patterns of behavior by the surrounding universal mind.

Independent from the duration we have actually chosen, the crucial point is that we exercise daily without interruption because this is how our sub-consciousness will be able to establish a new habit.

Regarding the effect even the duration of daily repetition plays an important role. Permanent repetition of an exercise, especially meditation, over a daily period of 40 days may break up old habits; and after 90 days new habits are integrated in our system. After120 days the new habit is a proven habit, so that we cannot return to old patterns. After 1000 days the new habit is mastered.

Meditations to the WAY OF THE HEART

The described meditations all originate from Kundalini Yoga according to Yogi Bhajan. If they are carried out daily for a period of 90 or 120 days (see aforementioned chapter) and under exact obedience of the instructions; they scientifically lead to the desired result.

In order to avoid uncertainty regarding proper execution please contact a local Kundalini Yoga teacher or contact me.

1. THE LAW OF MENTALISM

"THE ALL is MIND; The Universe is Mental."

The Kybalion

MASTER'S TOUCH MEDITATION

(KRI INTERNAT. TEACHER TRAINING MANUAL LEVEL I, ©
YOGI BHAJAN, Ph.D., originally taught by Yogi Bhajan on July 13,
2000)

Posture: Sit in easy pose or in a chair with a straight spine with a light neck lock (*Jalandhar Bandh*). Sit very saintly, like you are the greatest incarnation of Lord Buddha.

Focus: The eyes are slightly open, focused at the tip of the nose.

Mantra: From the navel, sing:

Aad Such, Jugaad Such, Hai Bhee Such, Nanaka Hosee Bhee Such.

You may sing or chant the mantra, but it must be done in a monotone. The "Suchhh" sound is emphasized as you pull the navel in on each repetition of the word. As you chant aloud, listen with your inner ear. Let the inner ear vibrate. Tune your inner ear so that the hammering of the hammer bones enables your brain to analyze the sound as you hear it.

Mudra: Mahan Gyan Mudra. Place the pad (finger print) of the right index finger (Jupiter finger) on the pad of the left index finger, right palm facing out from the body, left palm facing in towards the body, forming a 45 degree angle of the fingers pointing upwards. Other fingers are curled into the palms with thumbs over. Hold the mudra at the Heart Center with the shoulders relaxed.

Time: 11 minutes to 2 ½ hours

End: Inhale, hold the breath. Exhale; relax the mudra and the breath. Close your eyes and rest for 2 minutes.

Comments: The mantra translates as "Primal Truth, True for all Time, True at this Instant, Oh Nanak, Forever True. These are the four stages of truth that must prevail through one touch. It is recorded in the scriptures that this meditation is to be practiced for 2 ½ hours. However, it is up to you how long you practice. This is a personal sadhana and does not replace group sadhana in the Amrit Vela.

Yogi Bhajan about this meditation:

"In this kriya that I am giving you, you have to tune your ears. Not the outer ear – it will not help you – it is the inner ear. It has two bones on the side and the hammer, and if the hammer and the bones have a proper

hammering, then your brain can analyze and understand at the same time you are hearing. The mudra allows the Infinite energy to come through. Chanting the mantra stimulates the upper palate with the tip of the tongue, turning the thalamus and hypothalamus. Focusing on the tip of the nose causes the frontal lobe, which controls the personality, to become like lead. At one point the pain can become so unbearable, you cannot stand it. Then it 'breaks,' and you have found what you are looking for and that is forever. Nobody can take it away. To grow roots, you must open yourself up.

"As an apprentice to this process, you offer yourself in surrender to receive the Master's Touch. You stand on the root of the tree like a little bear, who reaches up to hold the trunk and climbs to the top-most branch to get to the beehive, unaware of bee stings — intent on getting the honey. He drinks the honey, is satisfied and descends to the grounds, falling through the branches which break his fall. After stretching and nurturing himself, the little bear remembers the taste of honey and the sense of achievement. He goes up the tree again and again, reaching that achievement in ecstasy, and nothing else matters.

"Life is a lie if you do not achieve your Self for yourself. That is your honey, your sweetness. You must achieve Infinity where your identity is such a non-identity that it merges in Everything. Once you are that, you bless everybody. You are honored and in bliss — limitless, with no confinement, no territory, no demands, no requests.

"In this process, you provoke, offer, surrender, achieve and descend. Provoke, because everything is provocation, either to control or to receive. Offer, because you must decide how to offer, or present yourself. Surrender, because when you surrender, your working self becomes zero, shuniya. Surrender is the highest power to gain all that you want to gain. Achieve, because once you have a sense of achievement and say, 'My God!,' if you convert that "My God!" into "My Soul!" you have already found God. You

have a soul — achieve it! When you find your soul or yourself you are com-
plete. Descend, because like a forklift, you may descend, go into the dirt and
move up. This descent is in the highest state of mind and spirit.

"When the Age of Aquarius comes and people seek you out, you will
have no time but to touch them and say, 'Bless you!' to bring the entire
psyche and being of a person into balance. That touch will create a state of
Aad Such, Jugaad Such, Hai Bhee Such, Nanak Hosee Bhee Such, Original
Truth, Truth through time, Truth now and forever Truth. These must pre-
vail through one touch. This mantra will give you the power of the Master's
Touch. And when you perfect this mudra with the Jupiter fingers touching,
chant the mantra in one sitting for 2 ½ hours — one tenth of your day — it
will bring you this Touch.

There is no power or magic on this planet that can stop it. It has a per-
mutation, combination, projection and power which brings the entire Pra-
kirti, the Existence, into the being of Purkha, the Divinity. All will be grate-
ful to you; you will find grace, respect, love and satisfaction that you are
serving the creation of God. Then you will see God in everybody, in your-
self, and in every facet of life. It will come true: "If you don't see God in all,
you don't see God at all.' You will see God."

2. THE LAW OF CORRESPONDENCE

"As above, so below; as below, so above."

The Kybalion

MEDITATION — HAST KRIYA — EARTH TO HEAVENS
(Reaching Me in Me, p. 54, YOGI BHAJAN Ph.D., 31. January 1996)

Posture: Sit in easy pose or in a chair with a straight spine with a light neck lock (*Jalandhar Bandh*).

Focus: The eyes are closed. Concentrate on your spine.

Breath: The breath will come naturally.

Mantra and Mudra: Extend your Jupiter (index) fingers on both hands. Lock the other fingers down with your thumbs. Time your movements with the tape Sat Nam Wahe Guru #2 by Jagjit Singh.

- Touch Jupiter fingers to the floor on either side of you when the ragi chants "Sat."
- Touch Jupiter fingers together over the top of your head when the ragi chants "Nam."
- Touch Jupiter fingers to the floor on either side of you when the ragi chants "Sat."
- Touch Jupiter fingers together over the top of your head when the ragi chants "Nam."
- Touch Jupiter fingers to the floor on either side of you when the ragi chants "Wah-hay."
- Touch Jupiter fingers together over the top of your head when the ragi chants "Guroo."
- Touch Jupiter fingers together on either side of you when the ragi chants "Wah-hay."
- Touch Jupiter fingers together over the top of your head when the ragi chants "Guruoo."

Time: 22 minutes

End: Inhale deeply, hold the breath for 10 seconds, exhale and relax.

Comments: The most graceful power and knowledge come from Jupiter. Jupiter controls the medulla oblongata, the neurological center of the brain and the three rings of the brain stem.

If you do this kriya for 22 minutes a day, you will totally change your personality. Power will descend from above and clean you out. Anger and obnoxiousness will disappear from your personality.

3. THE LAW OF CAUSE AND EFFECT

"Every Cause has its Effect; every Effect has its Cause; everything happens according to Law; Chance is but a name for Law not recognized; there are many planes of causation, but nothing escapes the Law."

The Kybalion

MEDITATION TO RIP OFF THE CAUSE AND EFFECT OF KARMA

(YOGI BHAJAN Ph.D., 12 February 2001)

Posture: Sit straight in a cross-legged position. Bring the hands into prayer mudra in front of your chest. Slide the hands up and down across the mounds of the hands in rhythm with the mantra. Be constant and consistent.

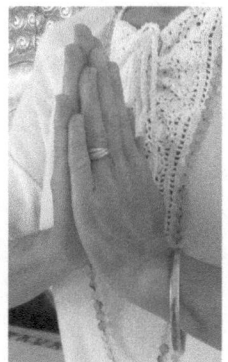

Mantra and Mudra: Chant "Sat Naam – Sat Naam – Sat Namm Jee, Wah-hay Guroo - Wa-hay Guroo – Wah-hay Guroo Jee" with the instrumental tape "Duni".

Time: Continue for 11 minutes.

End: To end, inhale deeply, hold, press the hands together as tightly as you can, and stretch the spine upwards. Exhale and repeat 2 more times. On the last inhale move the energy from the base of the spine to your crown and from the crown to your base 3 times. Relax.

4. THE LAW OF VIBRATION

"Nothing rests; everything moves; everything vibrates."

The Kybalion

HARI SHABAD MEDITATION

(YOGI BHAJAN Ph.D., 14. JUNI 1978)

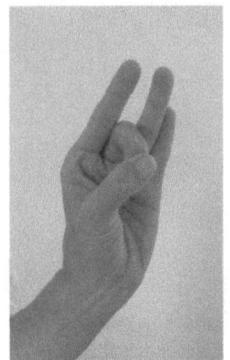

Posture: Sit in easy pose with a straight spine. Pull the chin in and push the chest out. Relax the arms down with the elbows bent and the forearms raised up from the sides of the body until they slant away from each side of the body at about a 30' degree angle. Sit with the legs crossed or in a chair with the weight of both feet equally distributed on the floor.

Focus: The eyes are 1/10th open.

Breath: Deeply inhale and completely exhale as the mantra is chanted.

Mantra and Mudra: Point the palms foreward and touch the Saturn or middle fingertip of each hand to its respective thumb tip. Leave the remaining fingers pointing up. Chant the following mantra three times as the breath is completely exhaled:

SAT NAAM HAREEE NAAM HAREE NAAM HAREE HAREE
NAAM SAT NAAM SAT NAAM HAREE

After the designated time is completed remain in the same body position and chant

SA-A-A-A-A-A-AT NAAM

Continue for a period of time. Then begin chanting

GURU GURU WAHE GURU, GURU RAM DAS GURU

three times per breath. Chant in a monotone very forcefully, stressing the first syllable of each word.

Time: Chant the first mantra for 31 minutes. Then chant the next mantras for as long as desired.

Comments: Pulling the chin in and pushing the chest out creates an equilibrium and prevents freaking out while meditating. The meditation "eliminates negativity, brings positivity, arouses the spirit to blossom," and when long SAT NAAM is done with it, it makes a combination that "has nothing parallel and equal to it." "HAREE" is the creative energy of God. "SAT NAAM" explodes it. It is of higher potency and multiplies the power of "HAREE" millions of times. If the third mantra is properly chanted, it will bring up the Kundalini.

5. THE LAW OF POLARITY

"Everything is Dual; everything has poles; everything has its pair of opposites; like and unlike are the same; opposites are identical in nature, but different in degree; extremes meet; all truths are but half-truths; all paradoxes may be reconciled."

The Kybalion

MERGER OF THE SUN AND THE MOON

(YOGI BHAJAN Ph.D., 22. APRIL 1977)

Posture: Sit in a comfortable meditative posture. Chin in and chest out.

Mudra: Bring the elbows in to the sides of the body and bring the hands palm up, fingers together, with the wrists bent back and the fingertips facing out to each side, parallel with the shoulders. Take care to maintain the hand position throughout the exercise.

Eyes: Tip of the nose; as you continue the meditation, the eyes should relax and may roll up.

Breath & Movement: Inhale and lift the left hand and shoulder up toward the ear, keeping the hand bent back and parallel to the floor. As you inhale, you will feel that the left nostril is more active than the right.

- Exhale through the left nostril and lower the hand, returning to the original position. Repeat on opposite side.
- Inhale and lift the right hand and shoulders up. As you inhale you will feel that the right nostril is more active.
- Exhale through the right nostril and lower the hand, returning to the original position.
- Continue to alternate sides and alternate nostrils, with a steady, evenly paced breath, not quick and not slow.

Time: 11 minutes. Can be increased with practice and experience.

End: Inhale and stretch the arms up, looking through the 10th gate. Exhale and relax.

COMMENTS: This movement serves to open the nostril on the same side, so that as you move alternate hands, the breath will also alternate from side to side.

6. THE LAW OF RHYTHM

"Everything flows, out and in; everything has its tides; all things rise and fall; the pendulum-swing manifests in everything; the measure of the swing to the right is the measure of the swing to the left; rhythm compensates."

The Kybalion

BREATHWALK WITH SA TA NA MA

(BREATHWALK: BREATHING YOUR WAY TO A REVITALIZED BODY, MIND AND SPIRIT, GURUCHARAN SINGH KHALSA and YOGI BHAJAN, JUNE 2000, © YOGI BHAJAN Ph.D.)

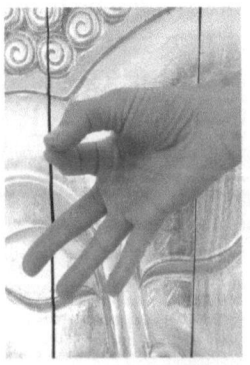

Posture: upright walking

Stand upright, centering yourself in your breath and take a few deep breaths. Start walking in a uniform, comfortable walking speed. Observe your body, feel every part of your body and notice where you feel well and where you feel tensions or pain.

Use this phase to correct your walking style if needed. Coordinate now your breath with your steps. Breathe into four equal parts through the nose in through four equal parts through the nose out.

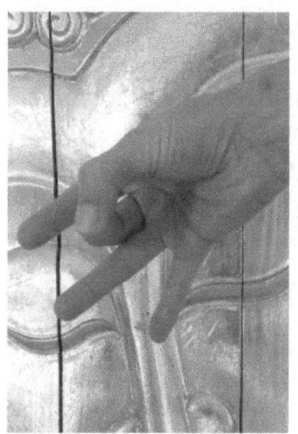 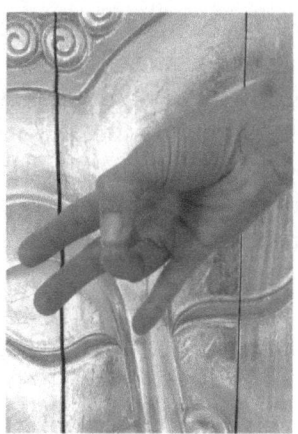

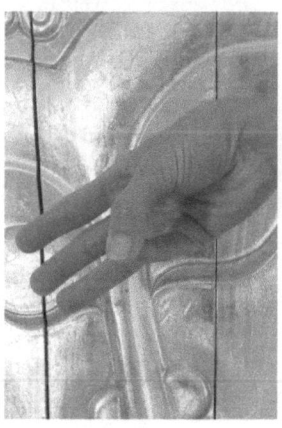

Add to this walking and breathing rhythm the mantra SA TA NA MA. Vibrate mentally with each breath segment and every step one syllable. Continue for three minutes. Then go ahead and breathe normally for five minutes. Then start again with the above described rhythm for five minutes, followed by three minutes of normal breathing. Then start again with the above described rhythm for 10 minutes, followed by a minute of normal breathing.

Become gradually slower and allow your senses to expand further during the exercise. End with stretching exercises.

Finally, sit quiet for a moment and imagine your skin with its sensitive surface. While you are breathing, feel how the surface of your skin breathes together with you. Imagine how this layer separates from your body. When you breathe in, feel how this layer expands away from your body. On the exhale feel how this layer relaxes and contracts. While you expand feel anything, let all in, every thought, every sound, taste, smell, every feeling and become very still.

While you keep on breathing, stretch the sensitive layer further out, initially only a few meters, then kilometers, light years up ad infinitum. Become more and more quiet with every breath and center yourself. Each inhalation makes you more alert and each exhalation relaxes you further. Remain in your heart.

Focus: If you want to go inside, center yourself and release your thoughts, concentrate on the point between the eyebrows (3rd eye). If you want to relax and gently energize, focus your attention on the tip of the nose.

Breath: synchronous with the walking rhythm - see above.

Mantra and Mudra: SA TA NA MA. With every syllable of the mantra touch one finger after the other with your thumb.

Time: unlimited

End: Inhale, hold your breath and stretch the layer of your skin as far as you can. After 10-15 seconds exhale quickly through the o-shaped mouth and let the layer quickly explode with the breath unto infinity. Be quiet, feel everything, bless everything and let go. Inhale, stretch your arms above your head and relax.

7. THE LAW OF GENDER

"Gender is in everything; everything has its Masculine and Feminine Principles Gender; manifests on all planes."

The Kybalion

ADI SHAKTI MEDITATION

(I AM A WOMAN YOGA MANUAL, © YOGI BHAJAN PH.D.)

Posture:

Part I: Sit in Easy Pose with the eyes closed, and the hands in Gyan Mudra. Meditate on the Infinite energy coming from the primal womb, in an unending spiral, without beginning or end, going to Infinity.

Part II: With the eyes closed, cup the hands with palms 4-6 inches (10-15 cm) apart, and in front of the face. Beam a mental light through them to the Infinite Light. Watch with mental eyes, through the hands, and see a beam of light going to Infinity. This is very mind-curing, and you will fall in love with it. Meditate with Long Deep Breathing.

Part III: Chant *Saa-Taa-Naa-Maa.* Go deeper into meditation. Guide your reason to go through the powerful imaginative circle you've created with your hands, like a huge beam of light from a torch. Keep the hands fixed in place.

Part IV: Maintain your position and concentration. Put your mind into that Infinite Light of its own ecstasy and chant the Kundalini Bhakti Mantra:

Mantra:

Adi Shakti, Adi Shakti, Adi Shakti, Namo, Namo

I bow to the Primal Power,

Sarab Shakti, Sarab Shakti, Sarab Shakti, Namo, Namo

I bow to the all encompassing Power and Energy,

Prithum Bhagvatee, Prithum Bhagvatee, Prithum Bhagvatee, Namo, Namo

I bow to that through which God creates,

Kundalini Maata Shakti, Kundalini Maata Shakti, Namo, Namo, Namo, Namo.

I bow to the creative power of the kundalini, the Divine Mother Power.

Mudra: Part I: Gyan Mudra (forefinger and thumb are touching each other, the other fingers are stretched), Part II: palms in bowl shape.

Time: All four parts of this meditation should be done for equal lengths of time. They can be practiced for 11, 31, or 62 minutes.

End: Inhale, suspend the breath for 10 seconds, exhale and relax the posture. Repeat for 2 times.

Comments: This mantra invokes the primary Creative Power which is manifest in the feminine. It calls upon the Mother Power. It will help you to be free of the insecurities which block freedom of action. By meditating on this mantra you can obtain a deeper understanding of the constant interplay between the manifest and the unmanifest qualities of the cosmos and consciousness.

8. The Law of Neutralisation

'The connection of the two polar oppositions in the zero point leads to the overcoming of separation, paving the way back to unity.'

MEDITATION FOR THE NEUTRAL MIND

(THE MIND – IT`S MULTIPLE FACETS AND PROJECTIONS, © YOGI BHAJAN PH.D.)

Posture: Sit in easy pose with the spine straight. Put both hands in the lap with the palms facing up. Rest the right hand in the left. The thumb tips may touch or not.

Focus: Remove all tension from every part of the body. Sit straight by achieving a balance. Close the eyes. Imagine seeing yourself sitting peacefully and full of radiance. Then gradually let your energy collect like a flow at the brow point.

Breath: Let the breath regulate itself into a meditative slow, almost suspended, manner.

Mantra: Concentrate without effort at that point and mentally vibrate in a simple monotone, as if chopping the sound, projecting each syllable distinctly:

Wha-hay gu-roo (Infinity identity from darkness to light)

Call on the higher self and keep going steadily through all barriers. Let go and let Cod.

Time: Practice this meditation for 17 to 31 minutes at a session.

End: Inhale, suspend the breath for 10 seconds, exhale and relax the posture. Repeat for 2 times.

Comment: It is easy to hear a truth and difficult to live it, to embed it deeply into your heart and mind. The Neutral Mind opens the gate to that deep remembrance of the self and soul. Jappa done with the refined Neutral Mind leads to Naam Chit Aveh. The Neutral Mind lives for the touch of vastness. It lets all other thoughts be without disturbance to your constant inner light.

9. The Law of Love

'The key stone of the pyramid is pure divine love in the form of Christos.

Any desire and all longings have been overcome; the being is resting in pure perception: Sat-Chit-Ananda (being-consciousness-blessedness). The heart unites what matter has separated; the return into the lap of God is achieved.'

WAY OF THE HEART

MEDITATION FOR PROJECTION AND PROTECTION FROM THE HEART

(KRI INTERNAT. TEACHER TRAINING MANUAL LEVEL I, © YOGI BHAJAN, Ph.D., 2003)

Posture: Sit in easy pose with light neck lock (*Jalandhar Bandh*).

Focus: Focus your eyes at the brow point.

Mantra:

AAD GURAY NAMEH
I bow to the Primal Wisdom.

JUGAAD GURAY NAMEH
I bow to the Wisdom through the Ages.

SAT GURAY NAMEH
I bow to the True Wisdom.

SIREE GUROO DAYVAY NAMEH
I bow to the great, unseen Wisdom.

Movement: Chant the *Mangala Charn Mantra*:

AAD GURAY NAMEH

As you extend the arms up to 60 degrees. Inhale powerfully as the arms return to the Heart Center and continue, extending them again as you chant,

JUGAAD GURAY NAMEH

Inhale, returning the arms to the Heart Center and chant,

SAT GURAY NAMEH

And repeat, chanting,

SIREE GUROO DAYVAY NAMEH.

Project the mind out as you chant. The full extension of the arms is timed to the chant.

Mudra: Place the palms together at the Heart Center in Prayer Pose. The thumbs are crossed.

Time: 11 to 31 minutes

End: Inhale, hold briefly, exhale and relax.

Comments: This meditation balances all your ten bodies, brings wisdom and protection and gives you an enchanting, magnetic personality, with many unexpected friends. This meditation is good for opening the heart chakra and sending the energy of love into the universe, thus creating the green energy that promotes prosperity. The *Mangala Charn* Mantra surrounds the magnetic field with protective light.

SAT NAM!

Additional Information

More information and ways to integrate this knowledge in everyday life are taught at seminars or in individual sessions.

Contact the Author

Gundula Puran Sukh Avenali lives in Italy and in Switzerland. She regularly organizes seminars on *"THE WAY OF THE HEART"* and also forms sporadically people to teach this as a path of enlightenment.

Dates for public seminars can be found on her website at

www.puransukh.com.

Gundula Puran Sukh also offers the opportunity to book individual coachings via skype or telephone on request. If interested, please send an email to **office@puransukh.com.**

Bibliography

The Kybalion: The 7 Hermetic Laws, The Three Initiates, Ospen Publisher

Kybalion: A Study of the Hermetic Philosophy of Ancient Egypt and Greece, Hermann E. Helmrich and Hans E Schwerin, 1997

The Emerald Tablets of Thoth the Atlantean, Urs Thoenen and Doreal, January 2002

Initiation into Hermetics, Franz Bardon, 2010

As above, so below - The 7 Laws of Life, Doreen Virtue

The magic key of the Kybalion: The Seven Laws of Life, Laura and Andrew Sherman and Friederike Berner, September 2009

Das Prinzip: Secret to creating the desired reality, Andreas Campobasso, July 2009

Himmlische Liebe, Gundula Schatz, Trinity Verlag, 2010

Love - Source of happiness, His Holiness the Dalai Lama, Herder Verlag

Singer, W. (2007) The search for the origins of wisdom and knowledge, from the "Mind and Life" conference 2005. Chökor, Tibet House Journal, Issue No. 44 (Tibet House Germany eV.), P.21 -27.

I Ching - The Book of Changes, Richard Wilhelm, Heinrich Hugendubel Verlag, 1956

The Flower of Life, Volume 1 and Volume 2, Drunvalo Melchize-dek, KOHA-Verlag, 2008

Pura Maryam Sophyah, www.puramaryam.de, work with light and love

The Vision of the Integral Yoga, Arjuna P. Nathschläger

The Life Divine, Sri Aurobindo, Sri Aurobindo Ashram Trust, 2006

Becoming One - The Psychology of Integral Yoga, A Compilation from The Mother`s Writings and Quotes from Sri Aurobindo, All India Press, Pondicherry, 2008

The Secret of the Veda, Sri Aurobindo, Sri Aurobindo Ashram Trust, 1956, 1998

Tibetan Yoga and Secret Doctrines, WYEvans-Wentz, Oxford University Press, 1935, 1968

Aquarian Teacher, Teacher Training Manual Level I, Kundalini Research Institute Internat., Yogi Bhajan, Ph.D. 2003

Authentic Relationships, Teacher Training Manual Level II, Kundalini Research Institute Internat. Yogi Bhajan, Ph.D. 2006

Meditations for the New Millennium, # NM0382, Kundalini Research Institute

Kundalini meditation, taught Siri Singh Sahib Bhai Sahib By Harbhajan Singh Khalsa Yogiji, # 46, 6/14/1978

Breathwalk: Breathing Your Way to A Revitalized Body, Mind and Spirit, Guru Charan Singh Khalsa Yogi Bhajan and, in June 2000

I Am a Woman Yoga Manual, Yogi Bhajan Ph.D.

The Mind - It's Multiple Facets and Projections, Yogi Bhajan Ph.D.

FSC
www.fsc.org

MIX

Papier | Fördert
gute Waldnutzung

FSC® C083411

Zeitfracht Medien GmbH
Ferdinand-Jühlke-Straße 7
99095 Erfurt, Deutschland
produktsicherheit@kolibri360.de